REFLEXリフレックス

REFLEX リフレックス
CONTEMPORARY JAPANESE SELF-PORTRAITURE
コンテンポラリー ジャパニーズ セルフポートレイト

004

イントロダクション 007 INTRODUCTION

キッド リフレックス 008 KID REFLEX
ホンマタカシ 010 TAKASHI HOMMA
梅佳代 020 KAYO UME
奈良美智 032 YOSHITOMO NARA
木村友紀 042 YUKI KIMURA
水谷孝次 054 KOJI MIZUTANI

ネイキッド リフレックス 062 NAKED REFLEX
北村公 064 KO KITAMURA
西村春海 072 SHUNKAI NISHIMURA
都築響一 080 KYOICHI TSUZUKI
長島有里枝 088 YURIE NAGASHIMA
宮下マキ 096 MAKI MIYASHITA

マンガ リフレックス 104 MANGA REFLEX
会田誠 106 MAKOTO AIDA
束芋 118 TABAIMO
ヤノベケンジ 126 KENJI YANOBE
根本敬 134 TAKASHI NEMOTO
水野純子 142 JUNKO MIZUNO

グループ リフレックス 152 GROUP REFLEX
吉永マサユキ 154 MASAYUKI YOSHINAGA
松下弘子 164 HIROKO MATSUSHITA
大竹伸朗 172 SHINRO OHTAKE
キュピキュピ 182 KYUPI KYUPI
三島正 190 TADASHI MISHIMA
若木信吾 200 SHINGO WAKAGI

アマチュア リフレックス 208 AMATEUR REFLEX
島尻武史 210 TAKESHI SHIMAJIRI
清水銈介 218 KEISUKE SHIMIZU
村川シゲ 226 SHIGE MURAKAWA
おのざわさんいち 234 SANICHI ONOZAWA

イマジン リフレックス 242 IMAGINED REFLEX
やなぎみわ 244 MIWA YANAGI
松蔭浩之 254 HIROYUKI MATSUKAGE
森村泰昌 262 YASUMASA MORIMURA

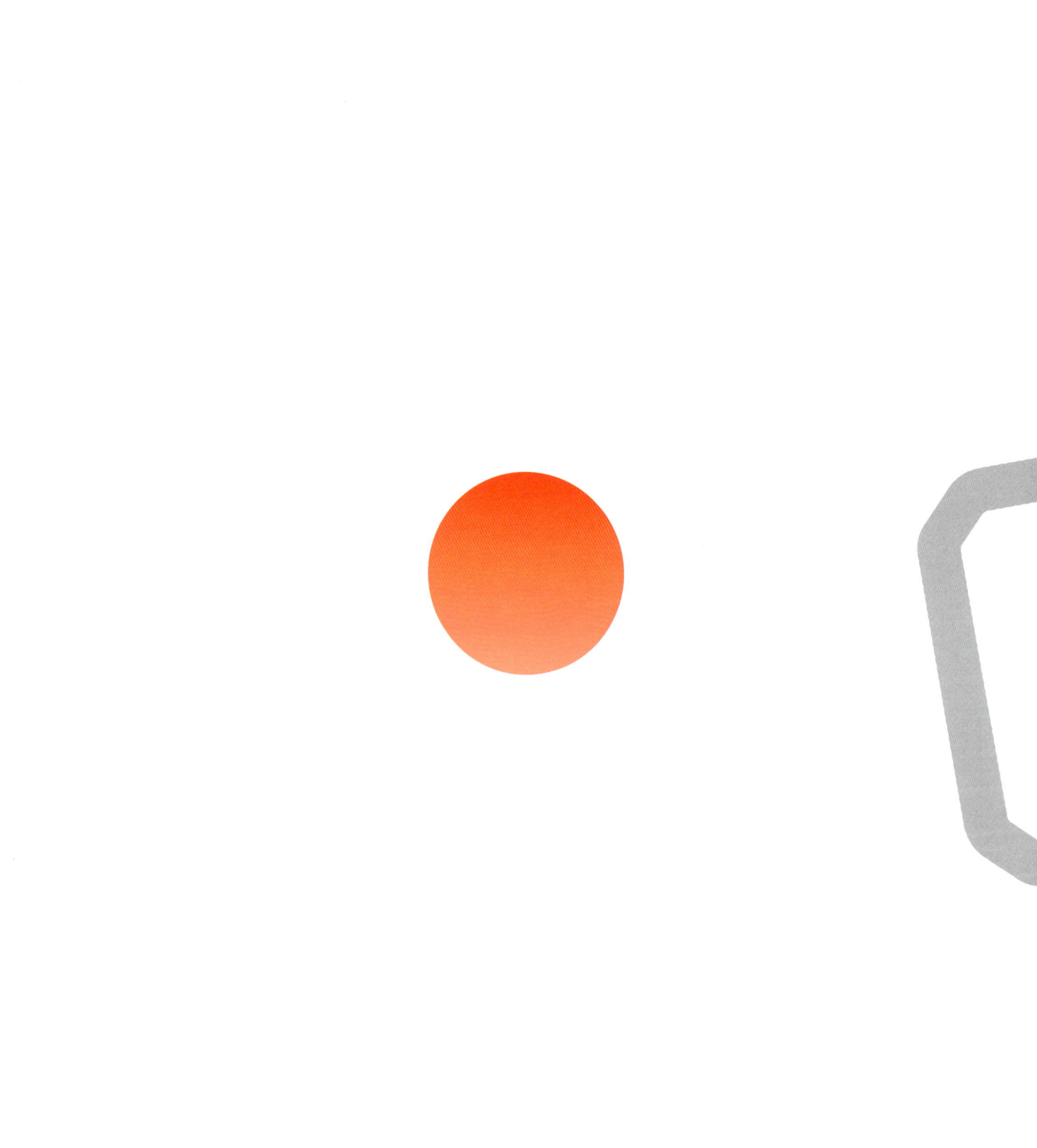

REFLEX リフレックス
CONTEMPORARY JAPANESE SELF-PORTRAITURE
コンテンポラリー ジャパニーズ セルフポートレイト

INTRODUCTION MARK SANDERS, FUMIYA SAWA AND KYOICHI TSUZUKI
イントロダクション マーク・サンダース／澤 文也／都築 響一

Ever since the Atom bomb first erased the cities of Hiroshima and Nagasaki at the end of the Second World War, the ideal of an indigenous Japanese culture based on traditional values was vaporised. In its place the Japan of the modern era witnessed the birth of a new mongrel aesthetic that today, six decades later, has flowered into a diverse and richly alternative popular culture that is as schizophrenic as it is quintessentially Japanese. From Elvis impersonators to gangs of marauding youth in the latest ad hoc street fashions, *Bosozoku* biker gangs to *Otaku* manga addicts; the cultural terrain that is contemporary Japan continues to change and mutate into ever more diverse and bizarre manifestations of itself. Yet in recent years the search for an identifiable Japanese sensibility has begun to be re-evaluated. In a hi-tech world saturated with consumer ideology, the question of a quantifiable Japanese identity has become of paramount importance. *Reflex* is a book that charts the alternative incarnations of the Japanese psyche as seen through the eyes of a new generation of Japanese contemporary artists, illustrators and photographers. All the work that is contained within this volume is produced by Japanese artists, both established and amateur, whose work represents a new mode of thinking about what it means to be Japanese in today's global village. Whether it is to be captured through the expressionistic outsider paintings of marginalised artists such as Sanichi Onozawa or the established art photography of Yasumasa Morimura, the bizarre amateur photographs of Takeshi Shimajiri or the disturbing manga fuelled paintings of Makoto Aida, each contributor to *Reflex* has been chosen for the way in which their work reveals a different dimension to the Japanese self that has hitherto remained hidden from the West. For contrary to popular opinion, Japanese society has moved away from the simple appropriation of Western popular culture to create its own unique brand of aesthetics that is often as surreal as it is insightful. *Reflex* is therefore but a glimpse into the soul of a modern Japan that finds itself in a constant state of flux. A diverse collection of reflexive portraits of the Japanese by the Japanese that aims to unravel the ways in which Japanese artists and photographers are currently rethinking and reconfiguring the world around them and beyond.

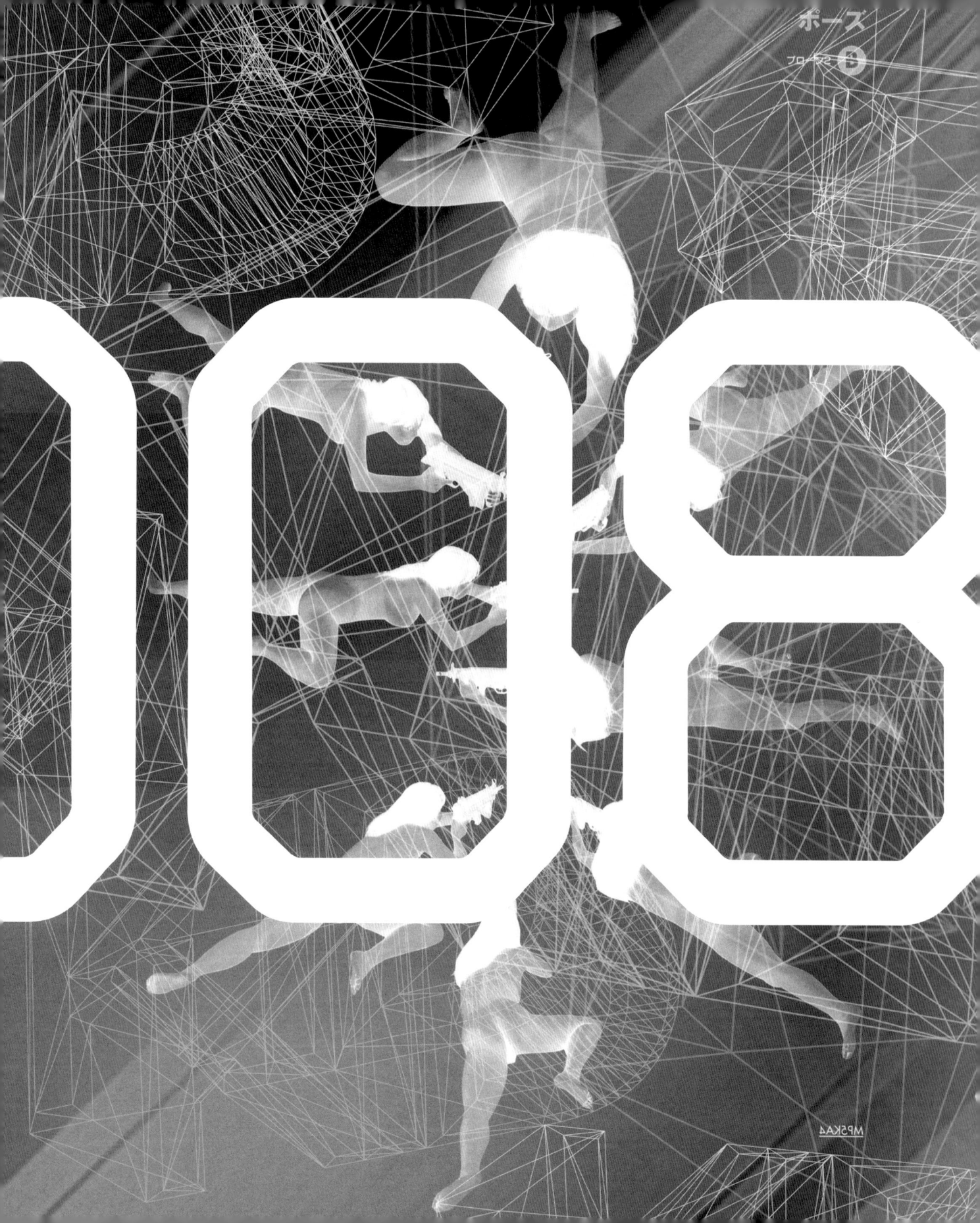

008-061 KID REFLEX

The unique state of being Japanese starts from childhood and being a kid in Japan could well be one of the most stressful experiences in the world. From an early age the pressure of succeeding in your education becomes the primary motivation of your life. From your first entry into *Shogakko* (Primary School) at six years of age to enrolment in a *Chugakko* (Lower Secondary School) at the age of twelve, *Kotogakko* (Secondary School) at fifteen and finally *Daigaku* (University) at eighteen, every hour of every day is dedicated to study. Extra lessons after school at a *Juku* (Cramming School) are not unusual and at all times school kids are required to dress in traditional uniforms in the guise of formal blue jackets and trousers for boys and 'sailor' outfits for girls. Within these rigid uniform restrictions many school kids find room to express themselves through a series of subtle fashion statements. Schoolgirls, for instance, have in the past created their own peculiar brand of 'sock fetish'. For over five years the trend was to wear loose white socks around the ankles, a fashion statement that spawned a countrywide Lolita complex in many adult males. Today the style is to wear tight blue socks that 'hug' the ankle. Yet apart from being a real (if innocent) source of youth fetish, Japanese kids are also a powerful economic consumer group. Many teenagers are given substantial amounts of pocket money by their parents as an incentive to study. As such they have become 'market controllers' for the vast entertainment industry that has developed since the 1980s. This collision of social responsibility coupled with the need to express oneself has culminated in the development of a constantly mutating youth culture that is as creative as it is fluid.

010 Takashi Homma's portraits of young kids in video arcades capture the essence of 'downtime' for many Japanese youth and reflect the artist's own childhood as a kid of the suburbs. The Japanese computer games industry is one of the largest in the world with giants such as Sony and Nintendo leading the way to more and more extreme versions of video game entertainment.

020 Kayo Ume's portraits of young girls and boys at play in Osaka (Japan's second city known for its anarchistic characteristics) reveal a more personal side of Japanese kids fooling around after school. In the first series, the boys pretend to be members of the *Bosozoku* bike gangs while the girls, again in traditional 'sailor' school uniforms, wear their first teenage bras on their heads.

032 Yoshitomo Nara started painting and drawing as a young child while his parents were away at work. His art therefore encapsulates his own lonely childhood and has since catapulted him to star status in Japan. Seen collectively his drawings reveal the pathological nature of childhood where violence and pop culture fuse together in a cute and popular style of execution.

042 Yuki Kumura's portraits of young teenagers pretending to be pregnant refer to the next generation of Japanese kids through teenage pregnancy.

054 Koji Mizutani's portraits of young girls smiling are taken from his popular publication *Merry*, which depicts some of the latest fashion trends from Japan's prolific street culture.

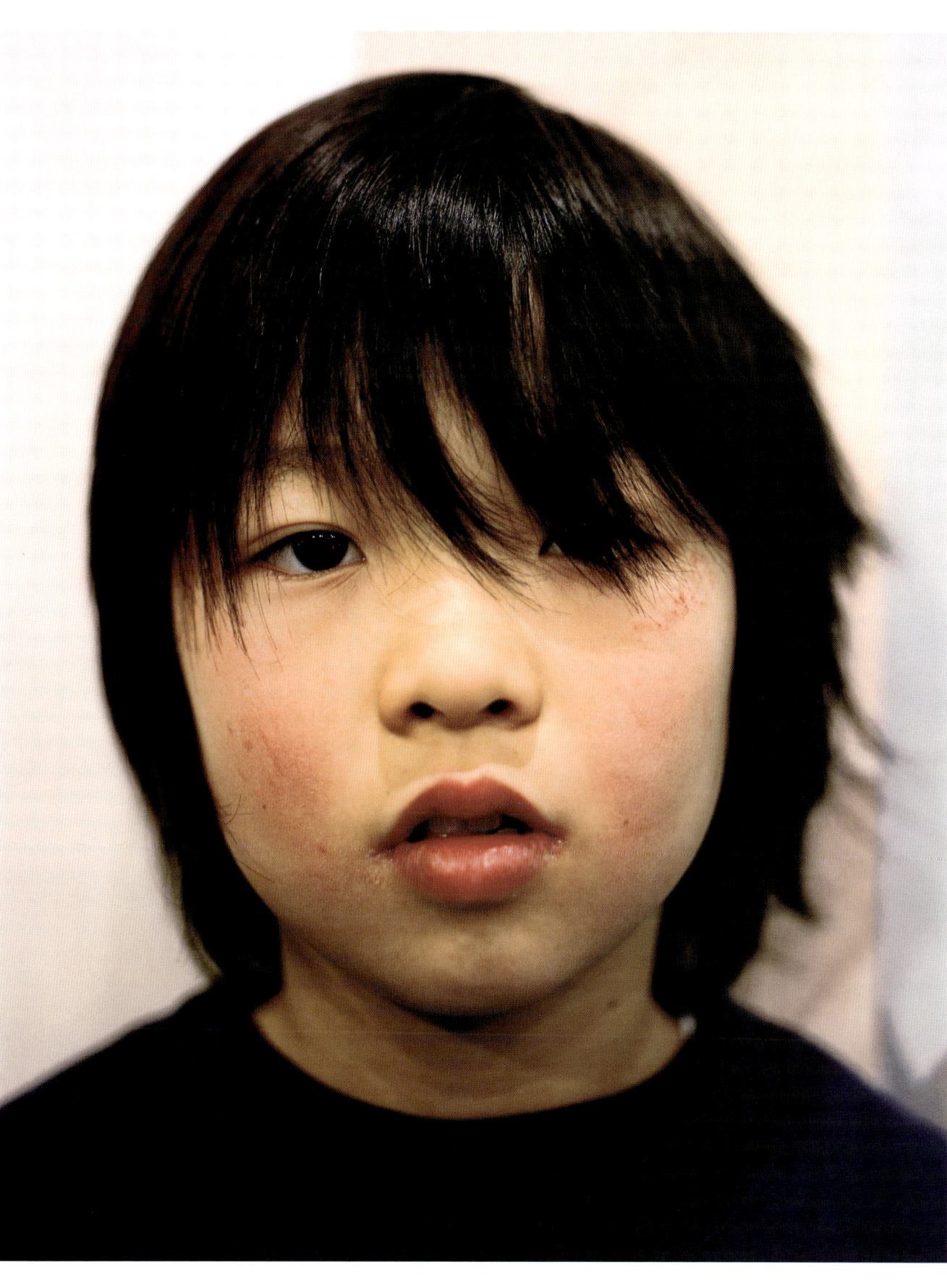

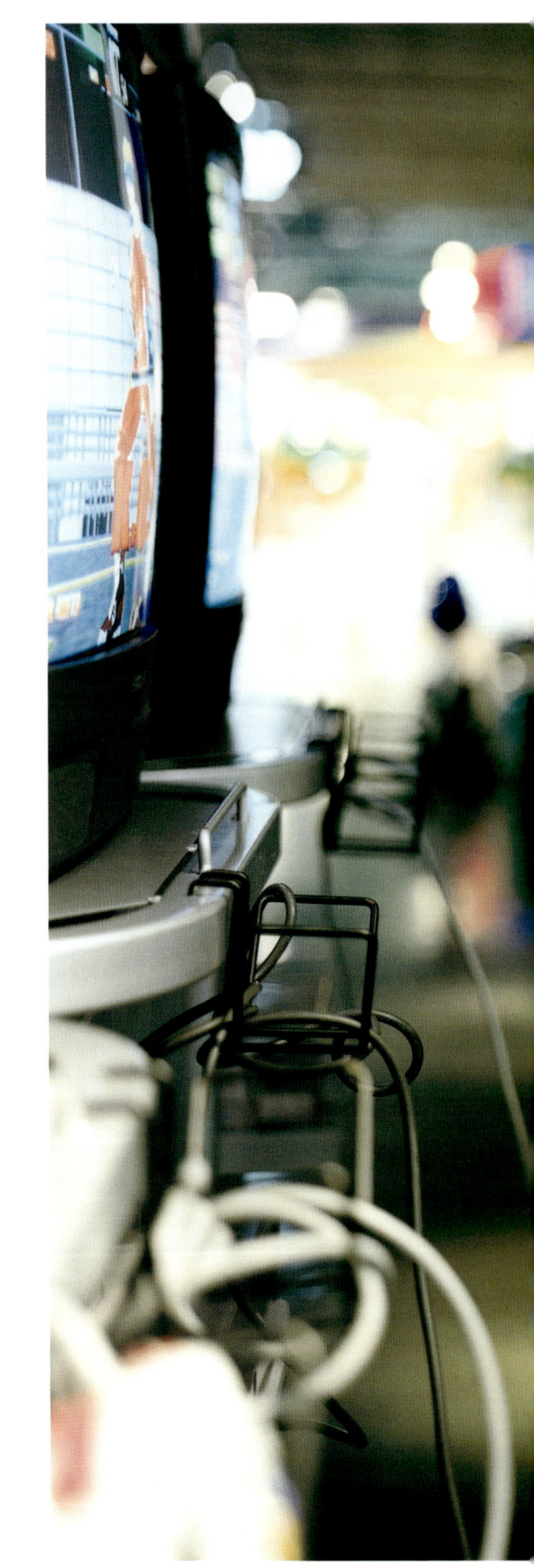

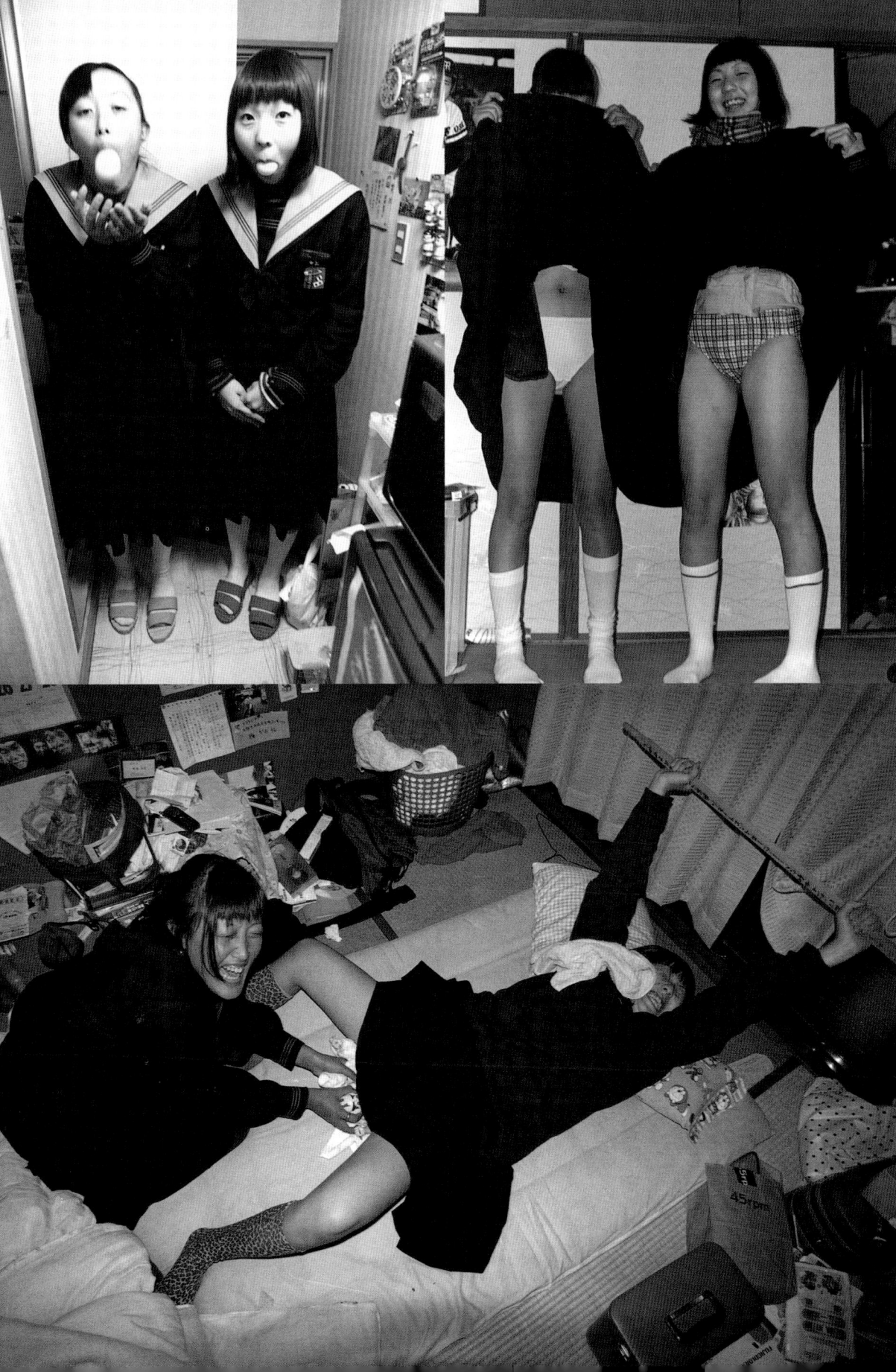

Liberty is laughing and shake your head!

KID REFLEX　木村友紀　YUKI KIMURA

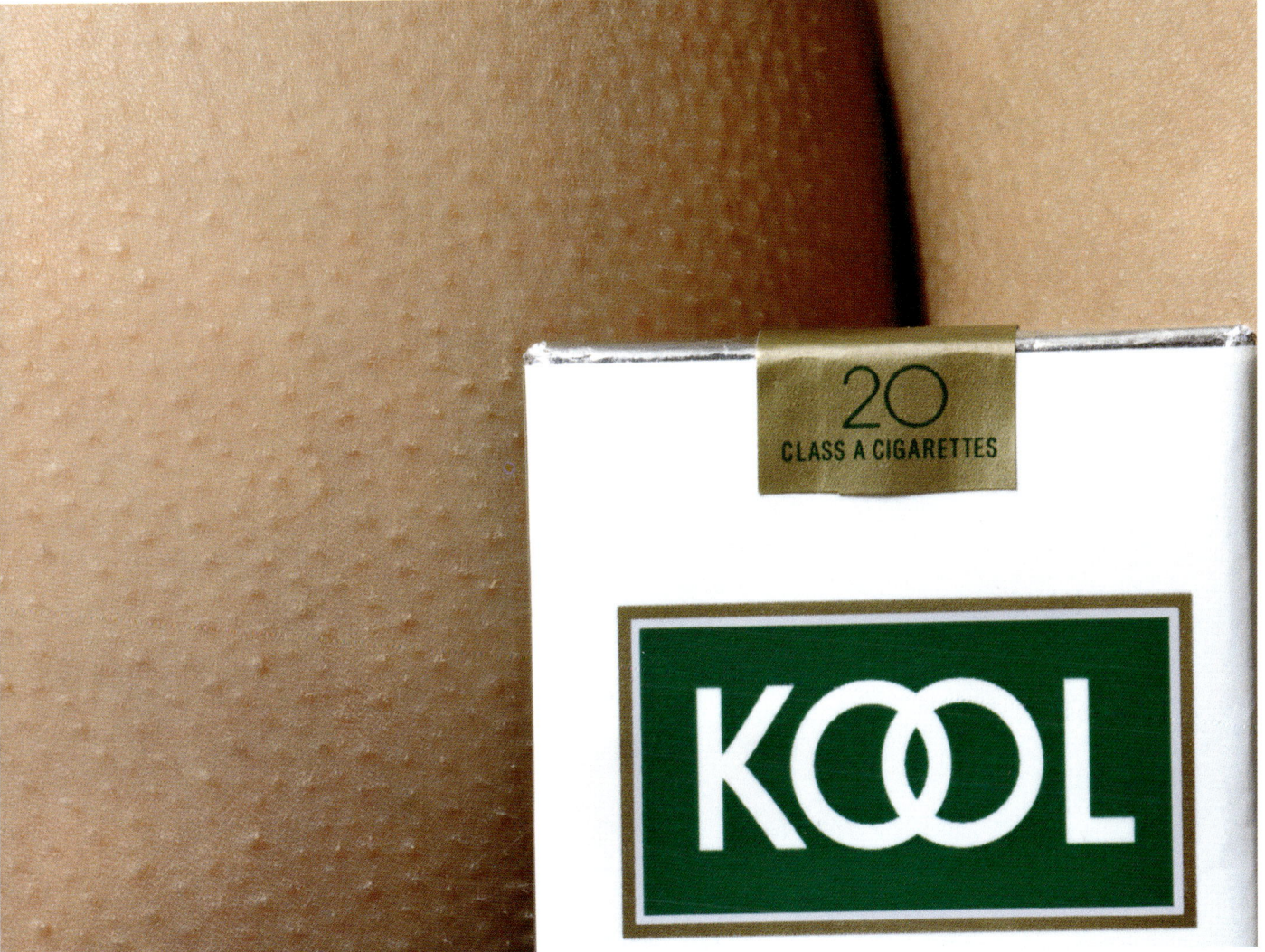

裸兵
前線キャンプで寝る Ⓑ

06

062-103 NAKED REFLEX

Being naked in Japan is a statement like no other. In a nation obsessed by uniforms raw flesh is the one body suit that continues to stand apart as a unique act of social and sexual defiance. Yet in the *Edo* period in the mid-18th century Japanese attitudes to the flesh were on the surface much more open than they are today. Mixed sex bathing was not unusual and there was a perceived difference between being 'naked' (which was considered a state of innocence) and being 'nude' (which was perceived as a conscious act). Indeed mixed bathing is still practised in certain provinces of Japan yet in a bizarre reversal of this traditional Japanese acceptance of the flesh, the current crop of Japanese obscenity laws are some of the strictest in the world and appear to be riddled with contradictions. Censorship is primarily intended to prohibit the public representation of sex in a nation that is by and large sex obsessed. Being nude in Japan is therefore much more of a 'public act' than it is a 'private matter'. The showing of genitals or pubic hair in Japanese or foreign magazines is highly censored and yet at the same time such censorship is strangely inverted. The laws on pubic hair are particularly vague with all hair being banned on images of minors, a fetish that spills out into the wider community. With the exposure of hair and sexual organs prohibited, the prolific Japanese sex industry has found ways to bypass the censors by using mosaics, blurring devices, negative pictures or even shaving off the hair entirely. There are also many self-published books that display nudity. The Japanese equivalent of page three in the British tabloid press is not a photograph of a naked girl but rather an airbrushed painting. Meanwhile, for many artists and photographers, being 'naked' as opposed to being 'nude' is considered to be a way back to a state of innocence.

064 *Ko Kitamura*'s portraits of young women completing acrobatics on their beds are taken from his self-published collection of erotic photography. For over 30 years he has been photographing his 'companions' in various states of undress.

072 *Shunkai Nishimura*'s illustrative paintings of nude females are the equivalent of page three models in British tabloid newspapers. These works are therefore intended to bypass the strict censorship laws of nudity by being 'illustrative paintings' as opposed to 'graphic photographs'.

080 *Kyoichi Tsuzuki*'s portraits of nude Japanese kids in their home environments allude to a private as opposed to public persona.

088 *Yurie Nagashima*'s self-portrait of herself with her naked family strips away the veneer of the traditional Japanese family unit.

096 *Maki Miyashita*'s portraits of young girls with their backs turned to the camera revert the aesthetic of popular Japanese fanzines in which teenage girls are photographed in their immaculate rooms.

NAKED REFLEX　北村公　KO KITAMURA

064-071

NAKED REFLEX　　KYOICHI TSUZUKI　　都築響一

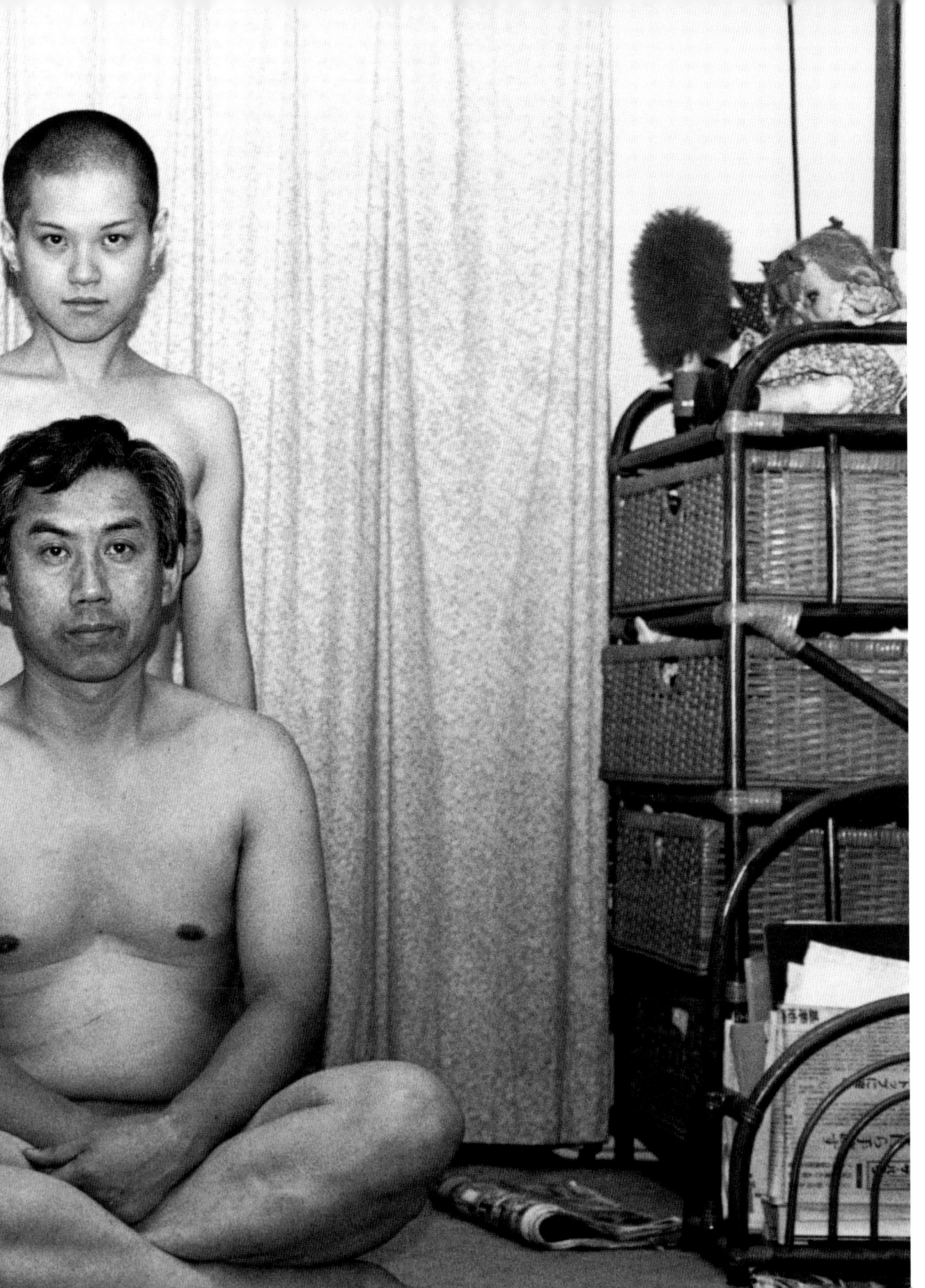

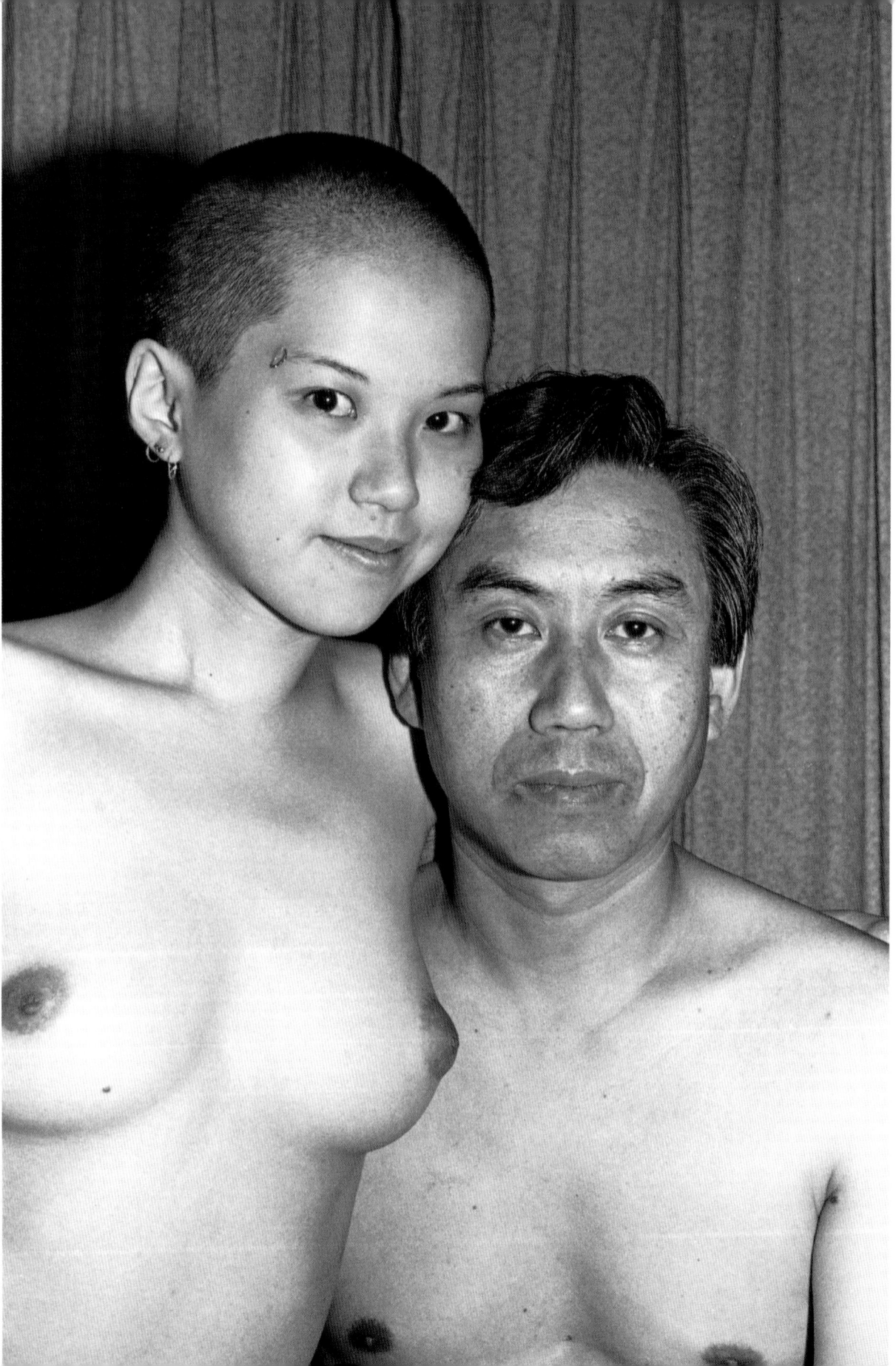

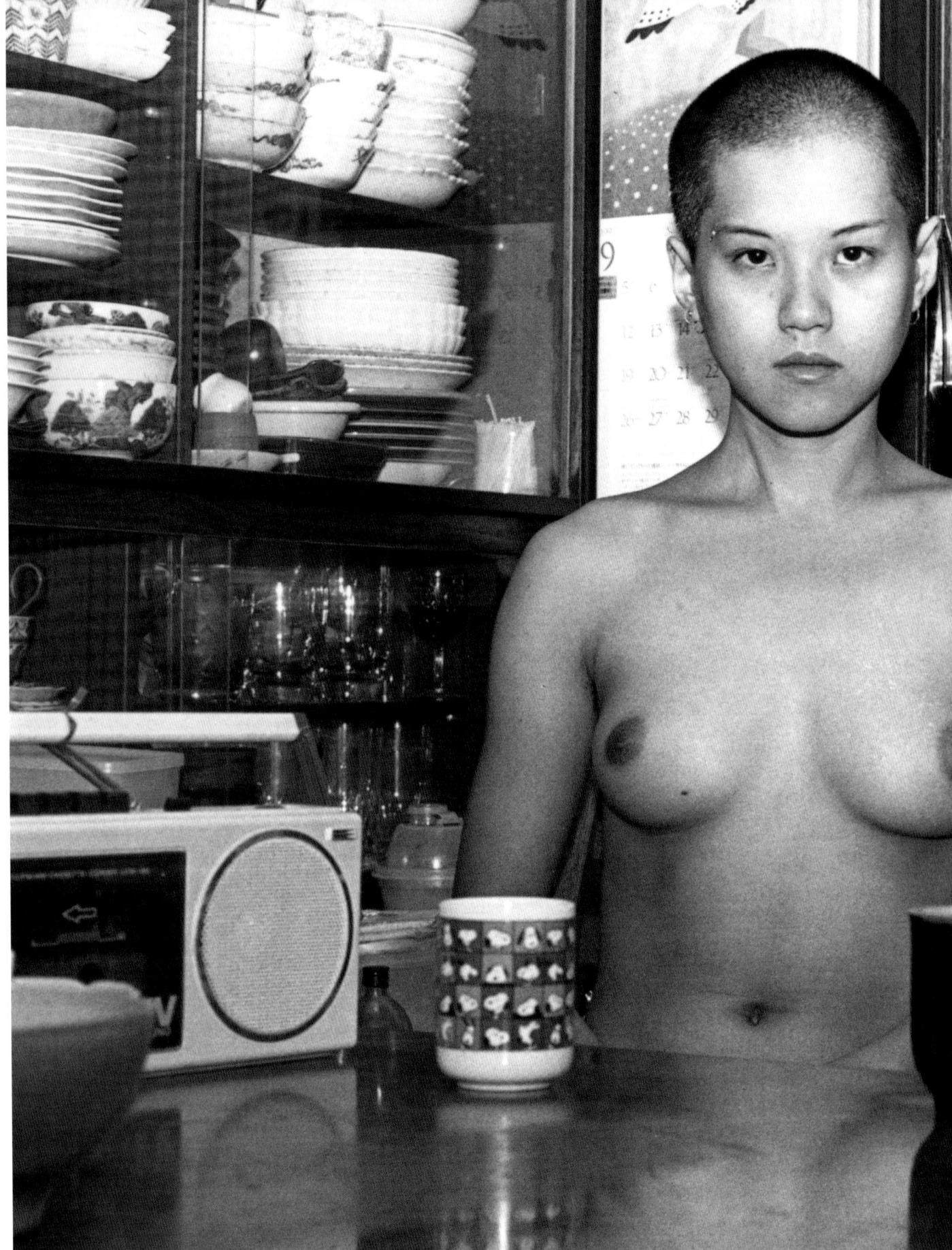

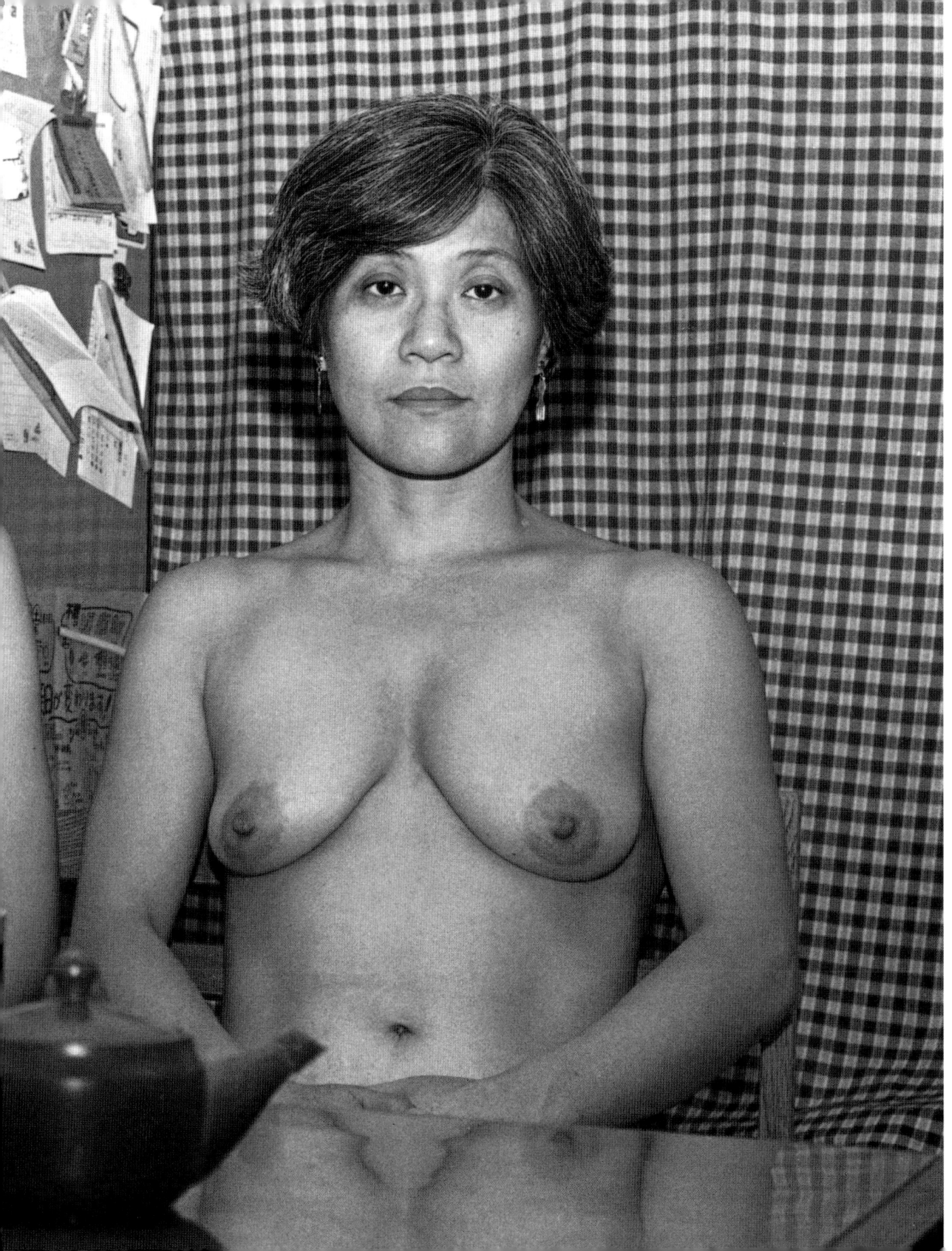

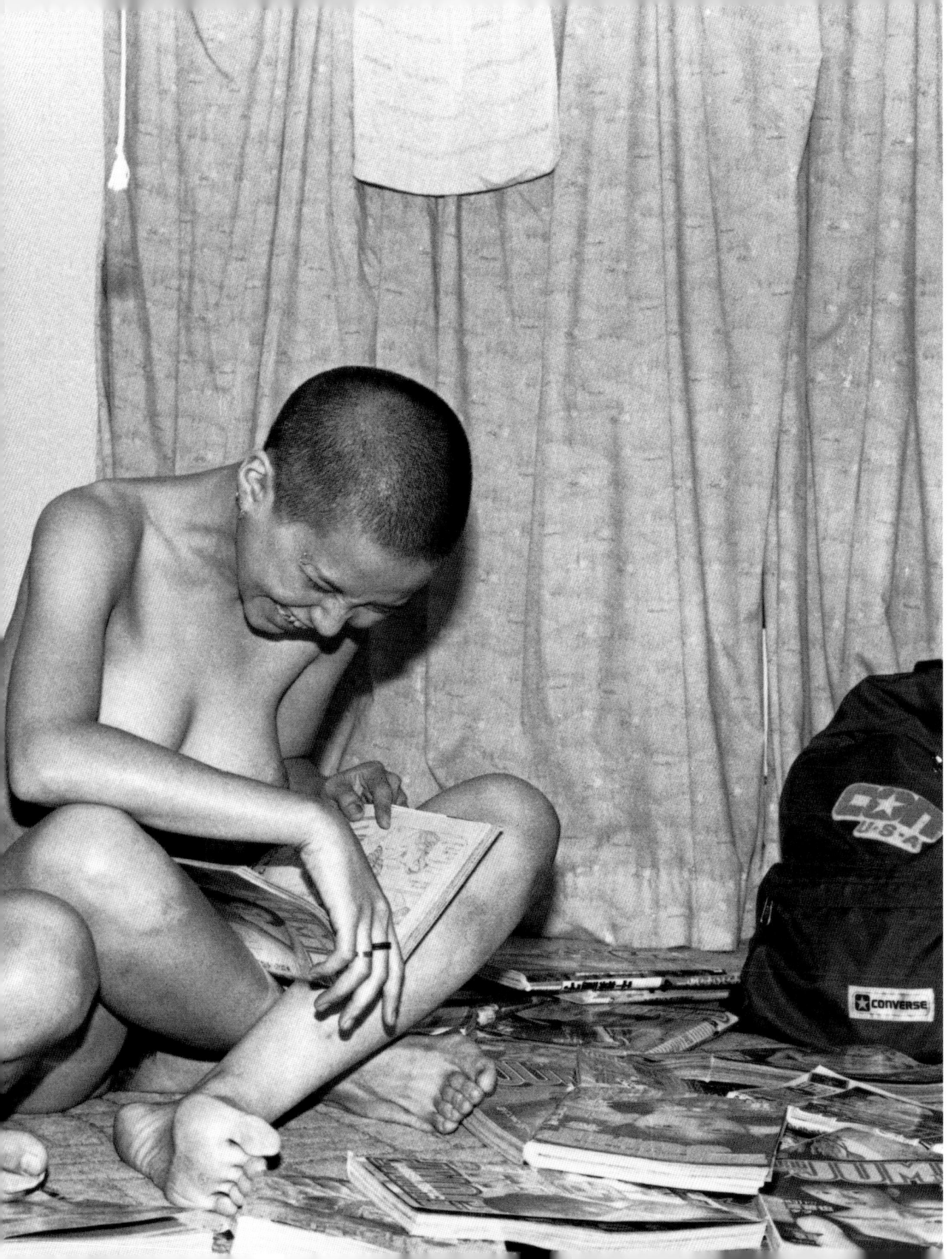

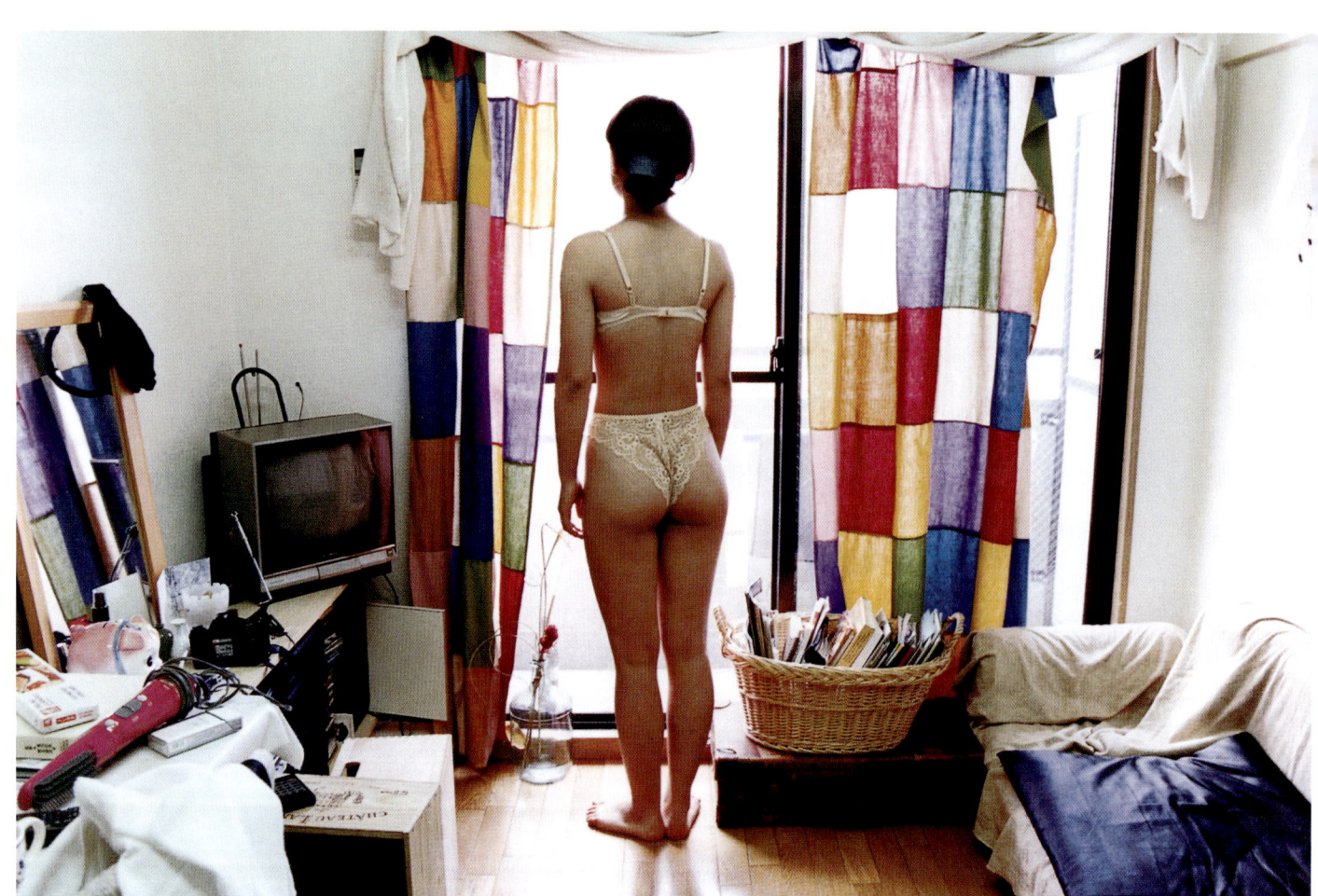

104-151 MANGA REFLEX

Manga in Japan is more than simply a visual aesthetic; it is an entire language device conceived through images and words. *Manga* magazines sell millions of copies a week and are considered by many Japanese to occupy a space somewhere between novels and film. The *manga* consciousness is therefore a form of animation that takes place in the mind and as such represents one of the most unique forms of mass communication in the world. Contrary to Western beliefs, *manga* is not only a form of entertainment but is also educational. Everything in Japan is expressed through *manga*, including popular novels, art criticism, political doctrines as well as economic commentaries. There are even *manga* books on medicine and other serious issues related to science that are targeted to a specific adult readership. At the same time, *manga* represents a whole philosophy of life or 'attitude' for Japanese kids. What is known as the *Otaku* generation in Japan are shy or withdrawn youngsters who have grown up within the media saturated world of modern Japan. The press often associate the term *Otaku* with the more violent strains of *manga* video games or comic book entertainment. They argue what is real all too often merges with fantasy and has even culminated in the famous case of a school boy cutting off the head of a fellow pupil and leaving it attached to the school gates in a macabre re-enactment of one of his favourite computer games. The multifaceted nature of *manga* has led many Japanese artists to explore the *manga* philosophy in their own working practice often with surprising results. In all cases *manga* becomes the Japanese equivalent of popular art.

106 **Makoto Aida** is a leading Japanese contemporary artist whose work often depicts the more sinister and violent side of the *manga* aesthetic; especially the male fantasy of female domination usually centred on young prepubescent schoolgirls.

118 **Tabaimo**'s fine art animations turn the traditional male orientated *manga* fantasy on its head by emphasising a suppressed vision of everyday life in Japan as depicted by two gay Sumo wrestlers fighting in a bathhouse. Her version of *manga* incorporates subtle references to the classic Japanese art of wood block painting whose gradations of colour she samples visually throughout her work.

126 **Kenji Yanobe**'s sculptural creations take as their inspiration the *manga* characters of his childhood such as Tetsuwan Atom (Astro Boy) and Godzilla. Fabricated out of scrap metal and a mishmash of other items, they operate as fully functional objects such as a radiation suit or floatation tank and are designed to be an outlet for the artist's own *manga* induced fantasies.

134 **Takashi Nemoto** is what might be termed an outsider *manga* artist who is now beginning to be taken seriously within the Japanese art world. His drawings form a link between *manga* and Western art as exemplified in the drawings of Otto Dix or André Masson.

142 **Junko Mizuno**'s form of *manga* fuses the cute style of Hello Kitty with the raw attitude of the *Otaku* to create a seductive mix of latent violence and innocence.

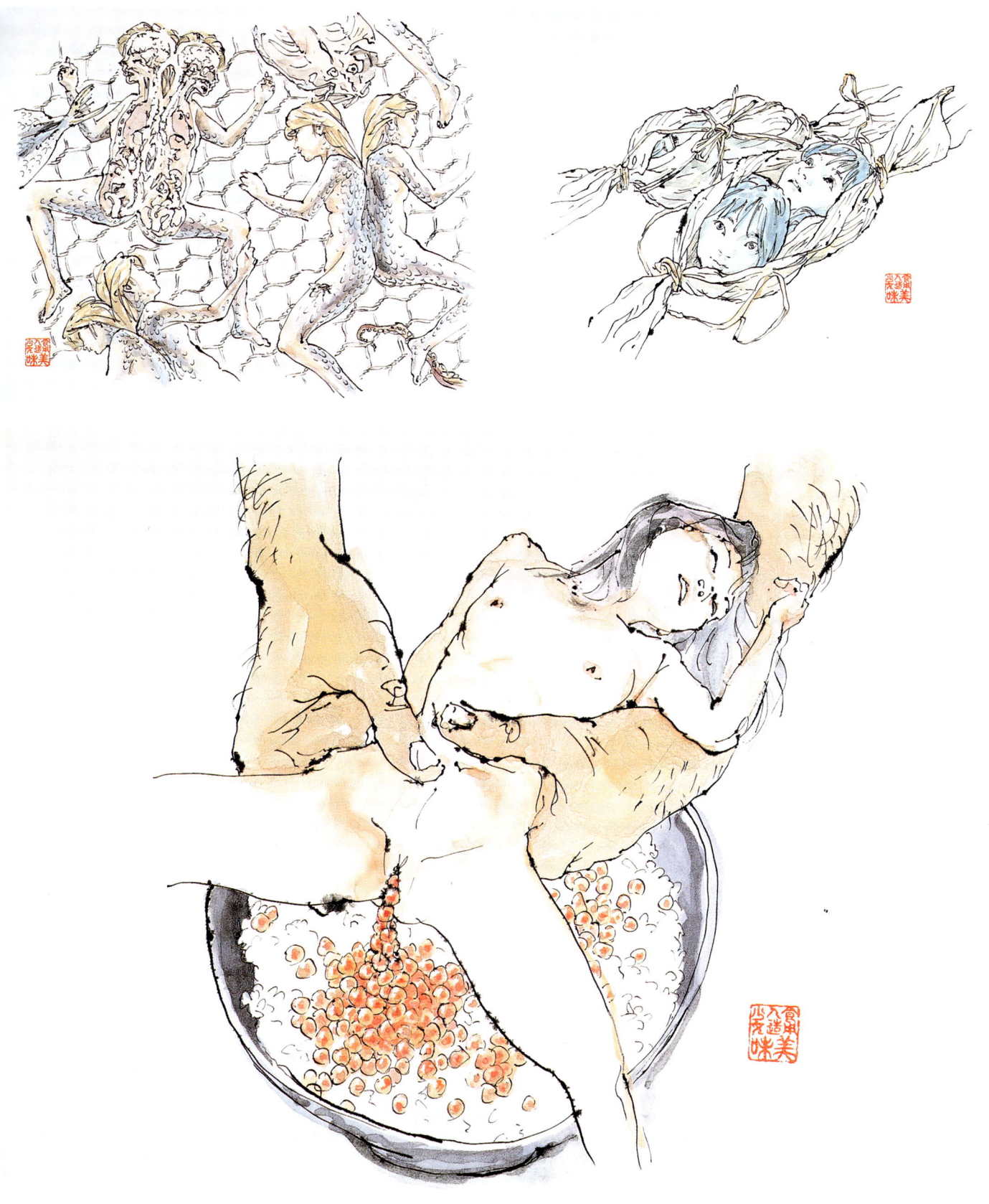

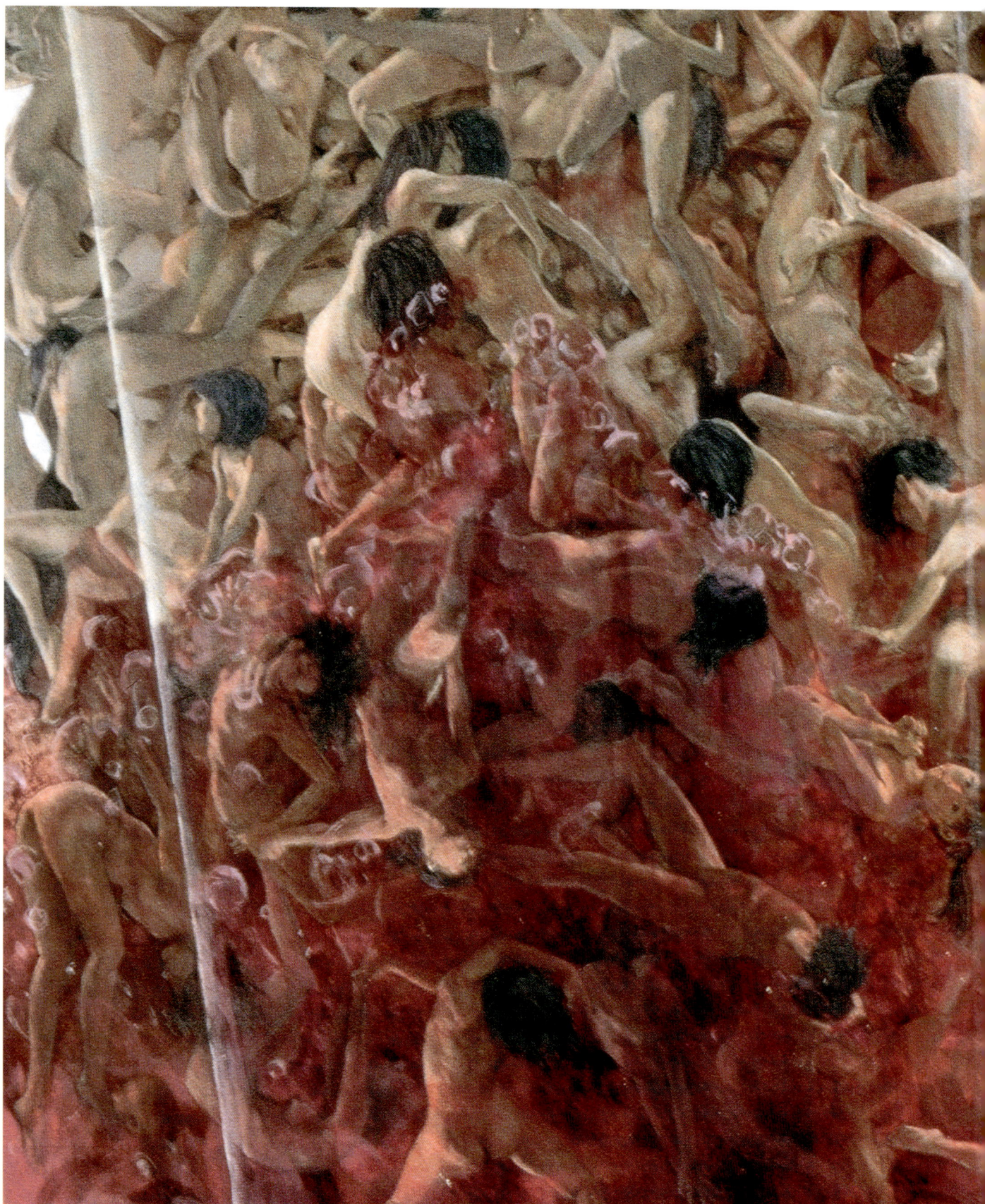

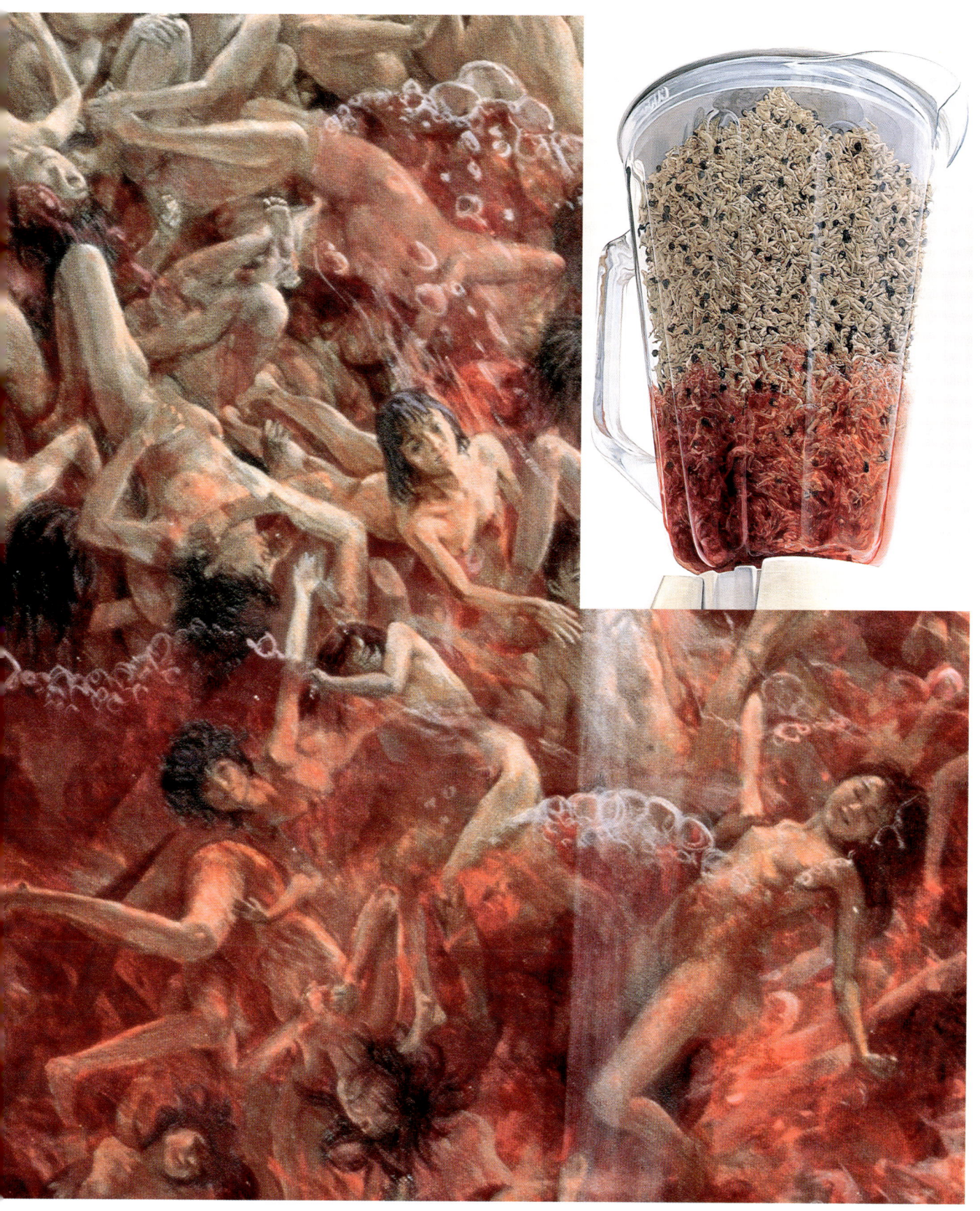

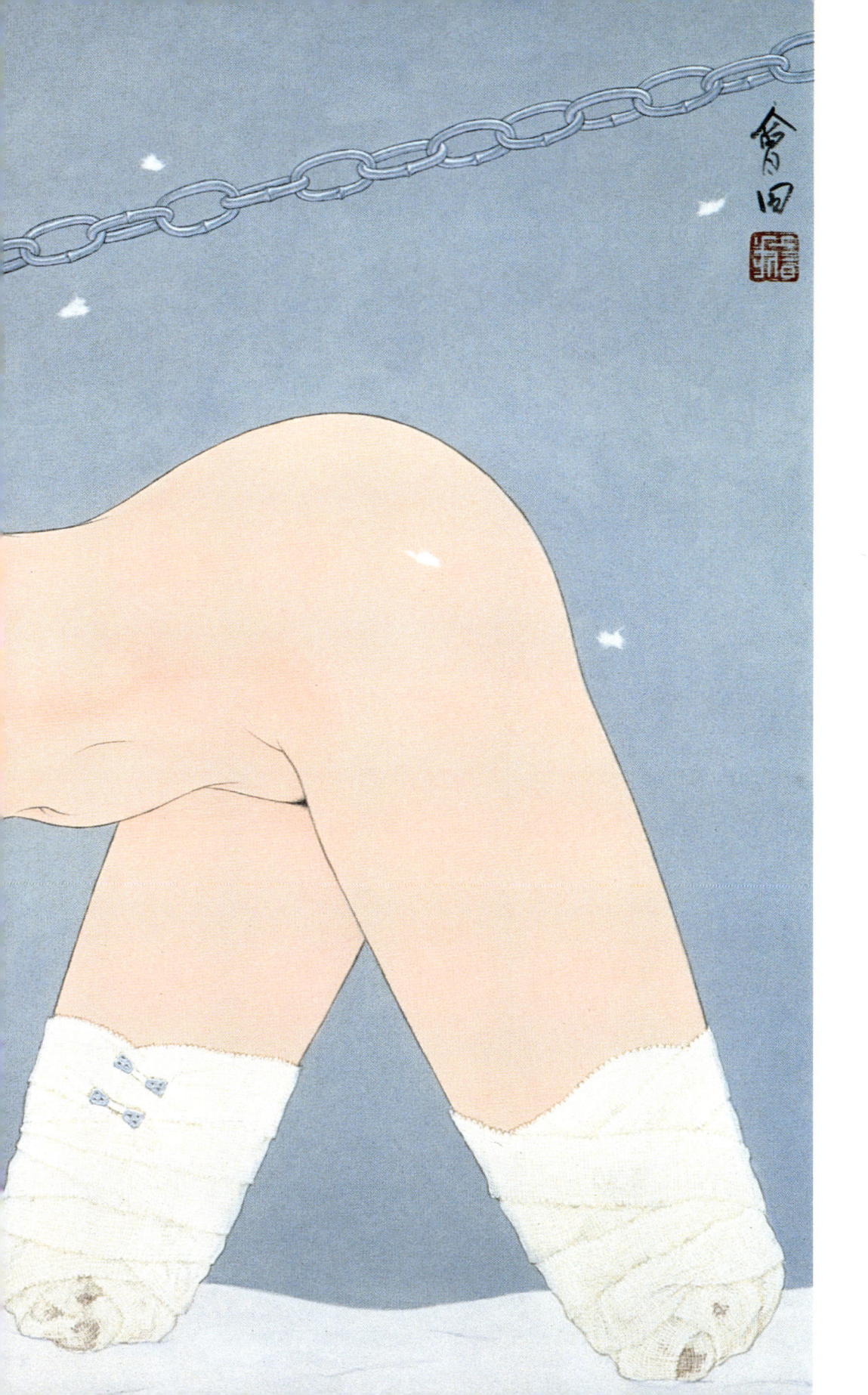

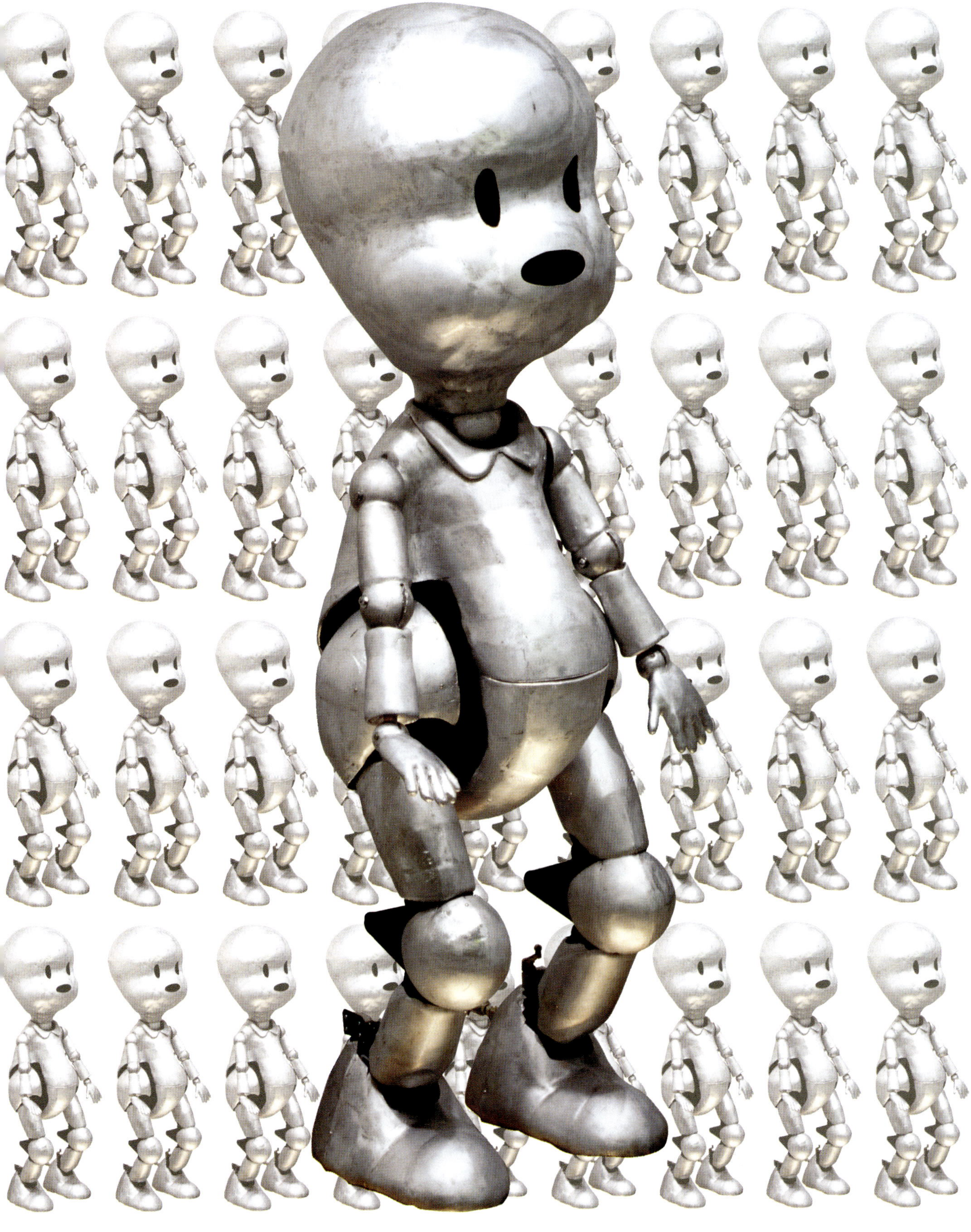

KENJI YANOBE

ヤノベケンジ

MANGA REFLEX

126-133

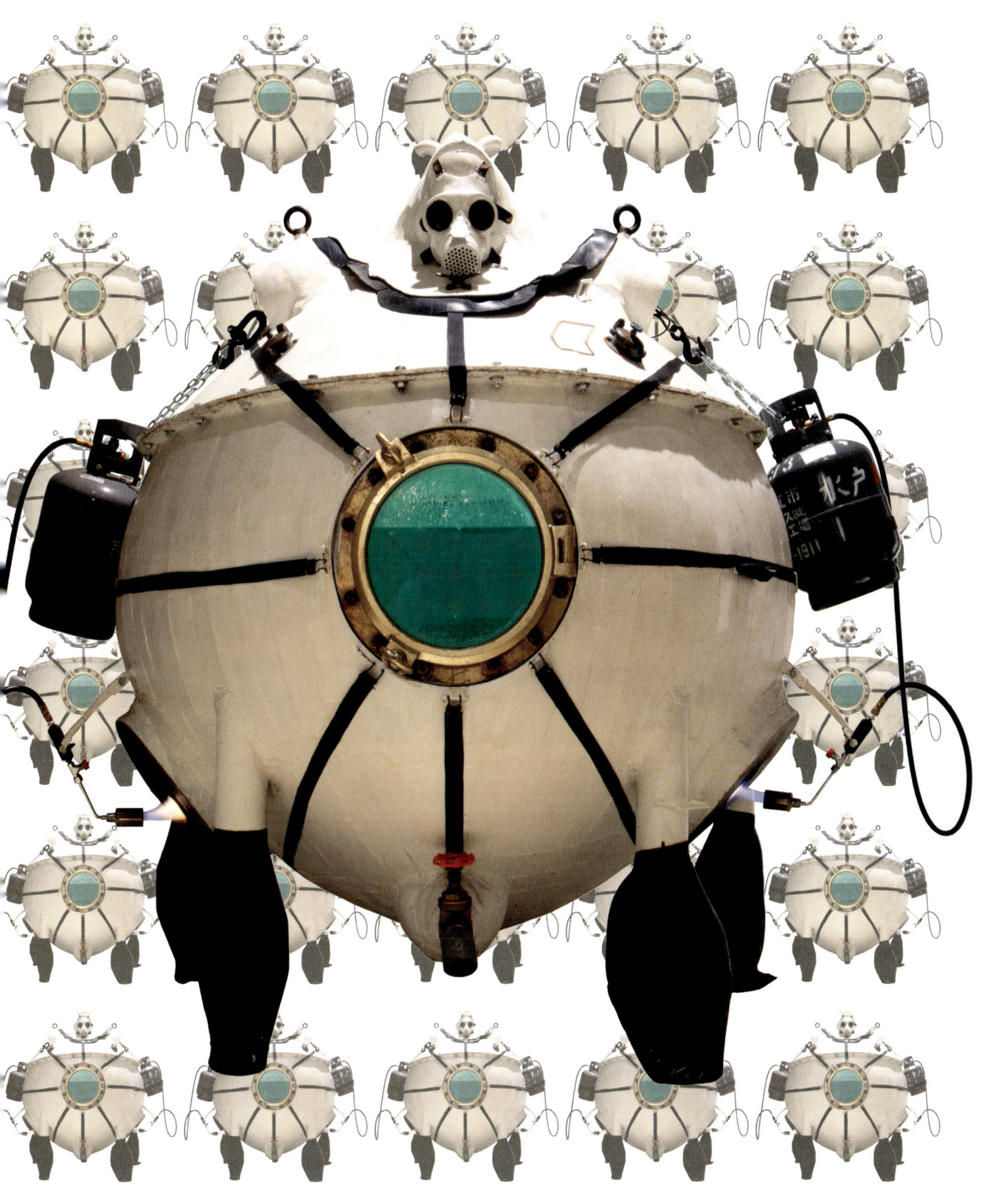

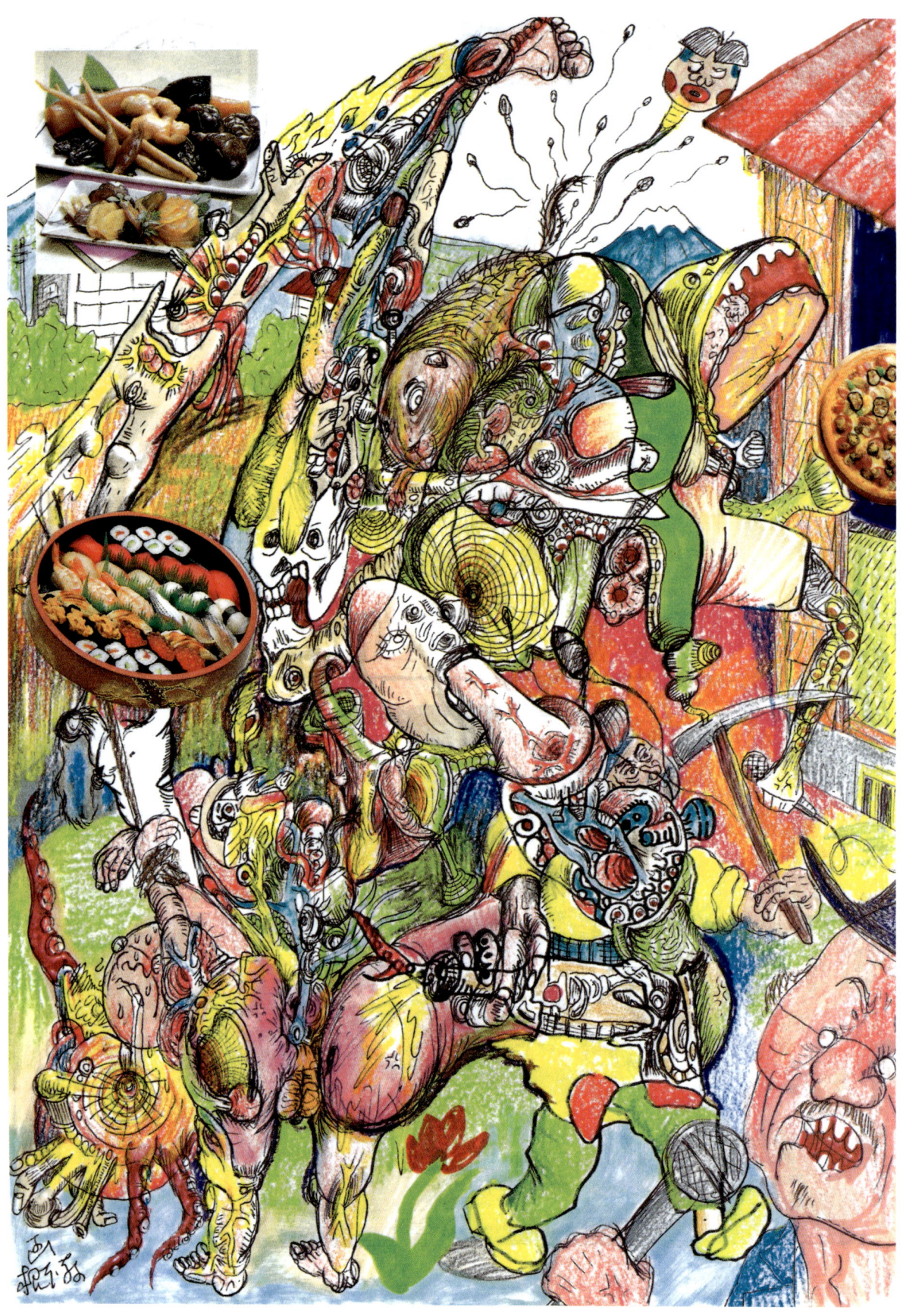

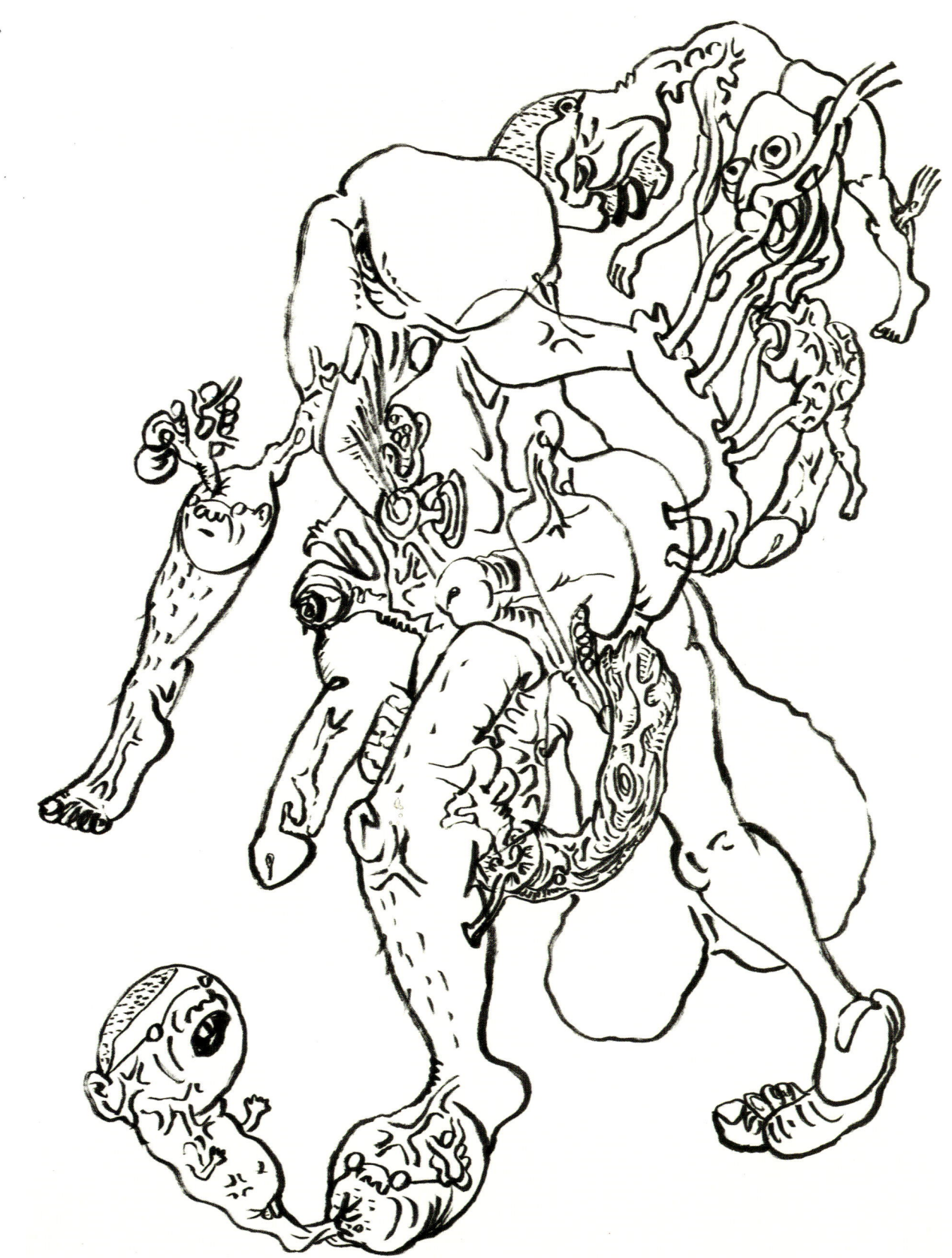

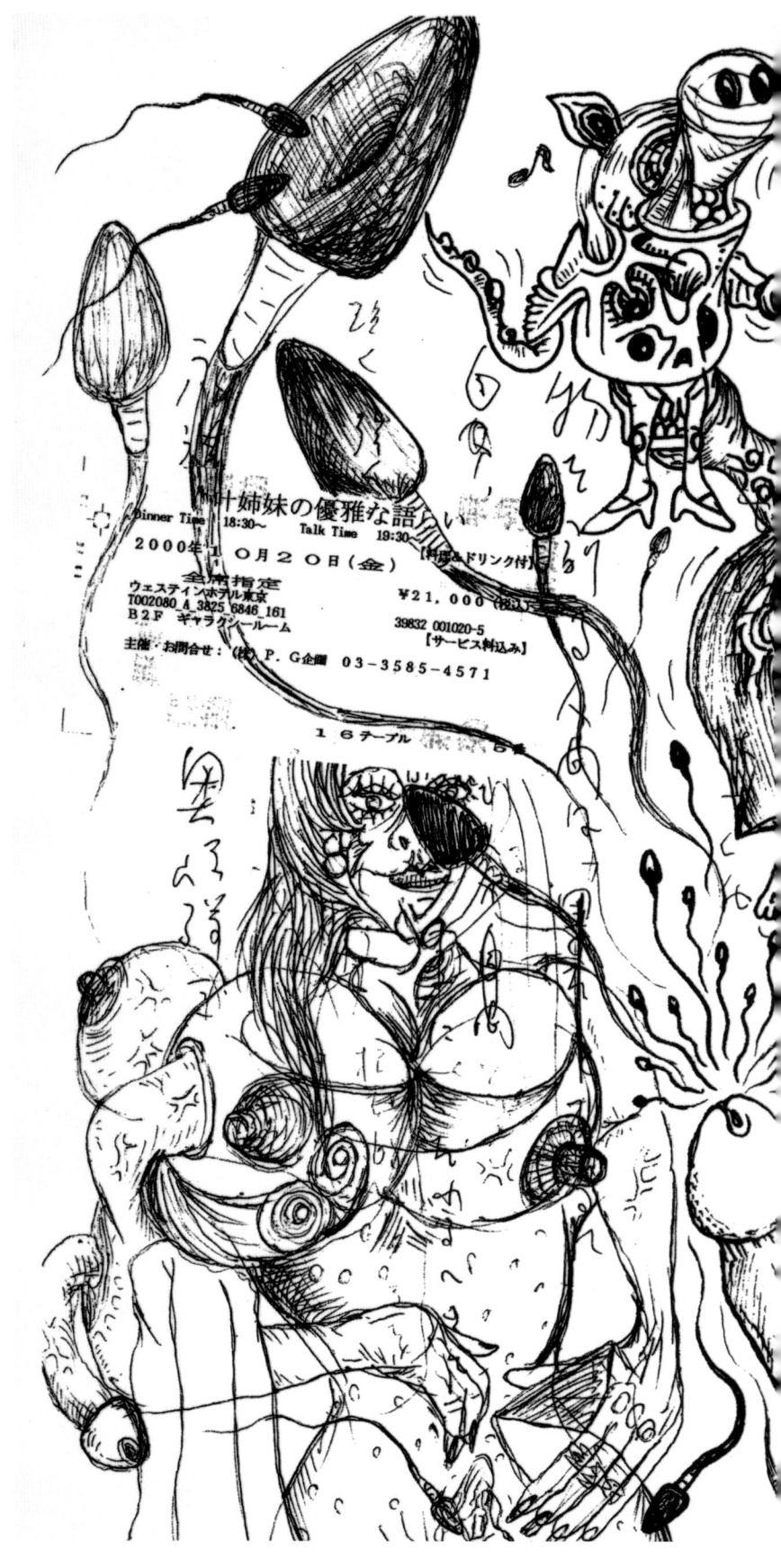

152-207 GROUP REFLEX

The ideal of belonging to a group is an essential part of Japanese society whether it is understood in the official sense of belonging to the culture at large such as office workers or as an alternative expression of group freedom as seen in the defined subcultures of the *Bosozoku* biker gangs or the *Yakuza* (Japanese Mafia). In all cases the collective expression of the group is paramount with the ideal of group conformity becoming an essential part of Japanese cultural life. Just as those belonging to the more authoritarian elements of society wear uniforms so too do differing youth groups model defined street fashions. The *Bosozoku* wear what is termed a *kamikaze* uniform which is the equivalent of the colours worn by Hell's Angels while Japanese Punks sport the standard leather jackets and PVC bondage gear. One of the most common sources of group identity for Japanese youth is to be found in various music subcultures. Belonging to a band is the epitome of the collective, a group consciousness that signals freedom of expression and individual liberty. Yet perhaps one of the most radical Japanese groups of all is the homeless, the true outcasts of Japanese society, who have developed their own unique methods on how to live and survive in Japan.

154 Masayuki Yoshinaga's intimate photographs of the *Bosozoku* or Japanese biker gangs reveals another side of Japanese youth that is little known in the West. Predominantly made up of young teenagers, both male and female, the *Bosozoku* are considered by many to be the reserve army of the *Yakuza* or Japanese Mafia although only a small percentage go on to a life in crime.

164 Hiroko Matsushita is a 70-year-old self-taught photographer whose portraits of the Japanese indigenous Punk scene have earned her many admirers. Her books on Japanese rock music have even culminated in her becoming an honouree Punk although she often finds the music too loud for her tastes.

172 Shinro Ohtake is one of Japan's most respected artists whose fusion of Pop Art and music have made him a hero with the younger generation and led to collaborations with such prestigious musicians as Eye of the noise band The Boredoms. His seminal piece *Dub-Hei and New Chanel* is a fictitious automated noise band that is run entirely by the energy generated by a second-hand electric motor that was originally used for a massage chair.

182 Kyupi Kyupi are Japan's leading cabaret group whose various antics are performed both as theatre and as live performances filmed for mass television audiences.

190 Tadashi Mishima's portraits of Japanese civil servants, from accident and emergency to air traffic control, reveal a group mentality that is encapsulated by the uniforms worn by each employee.

200 Shingo Wakagi meanwhile uncovers another group, that of the elderly and anarchic homeless in Osaka, who are more often than not marginalised by Japanese society.

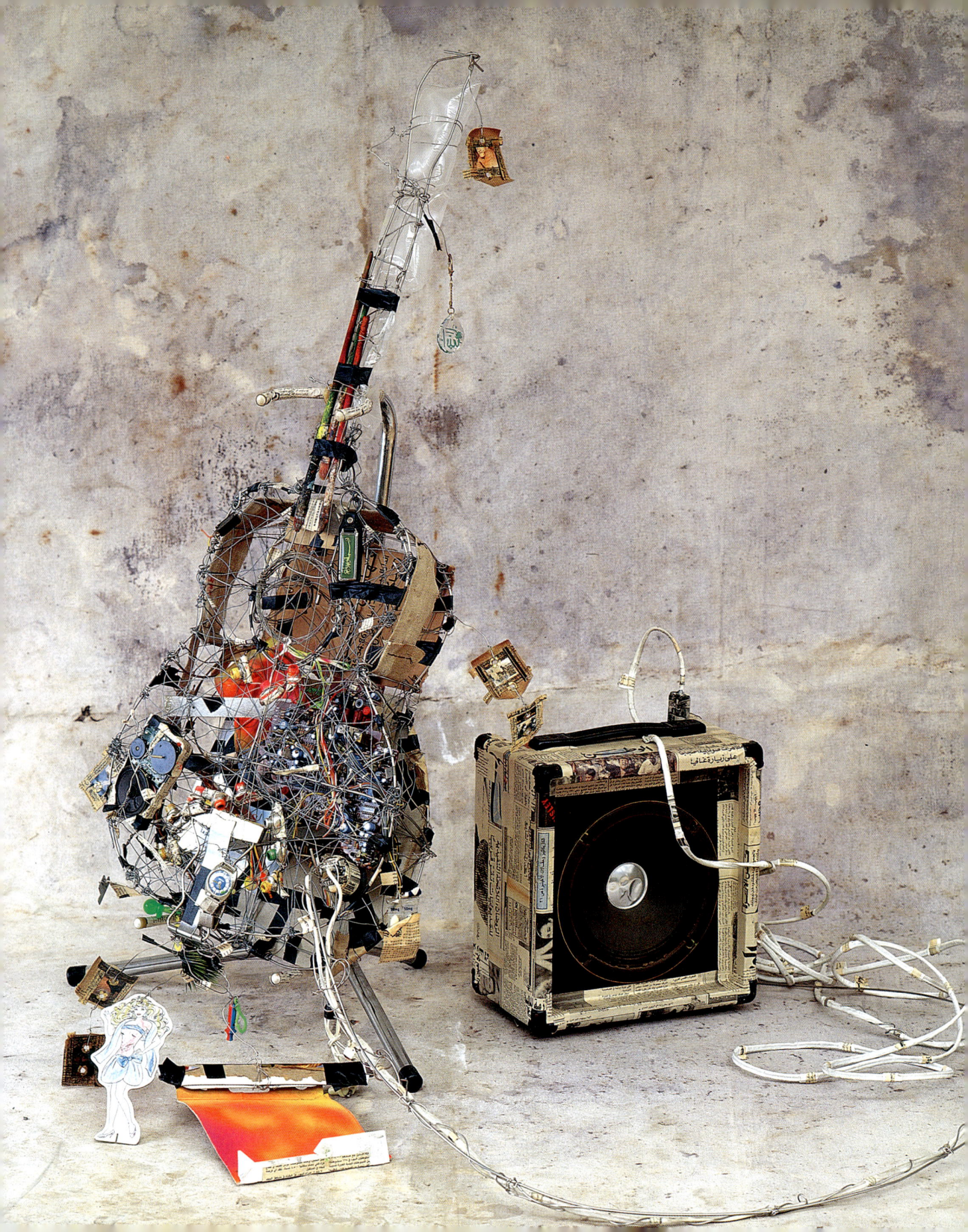

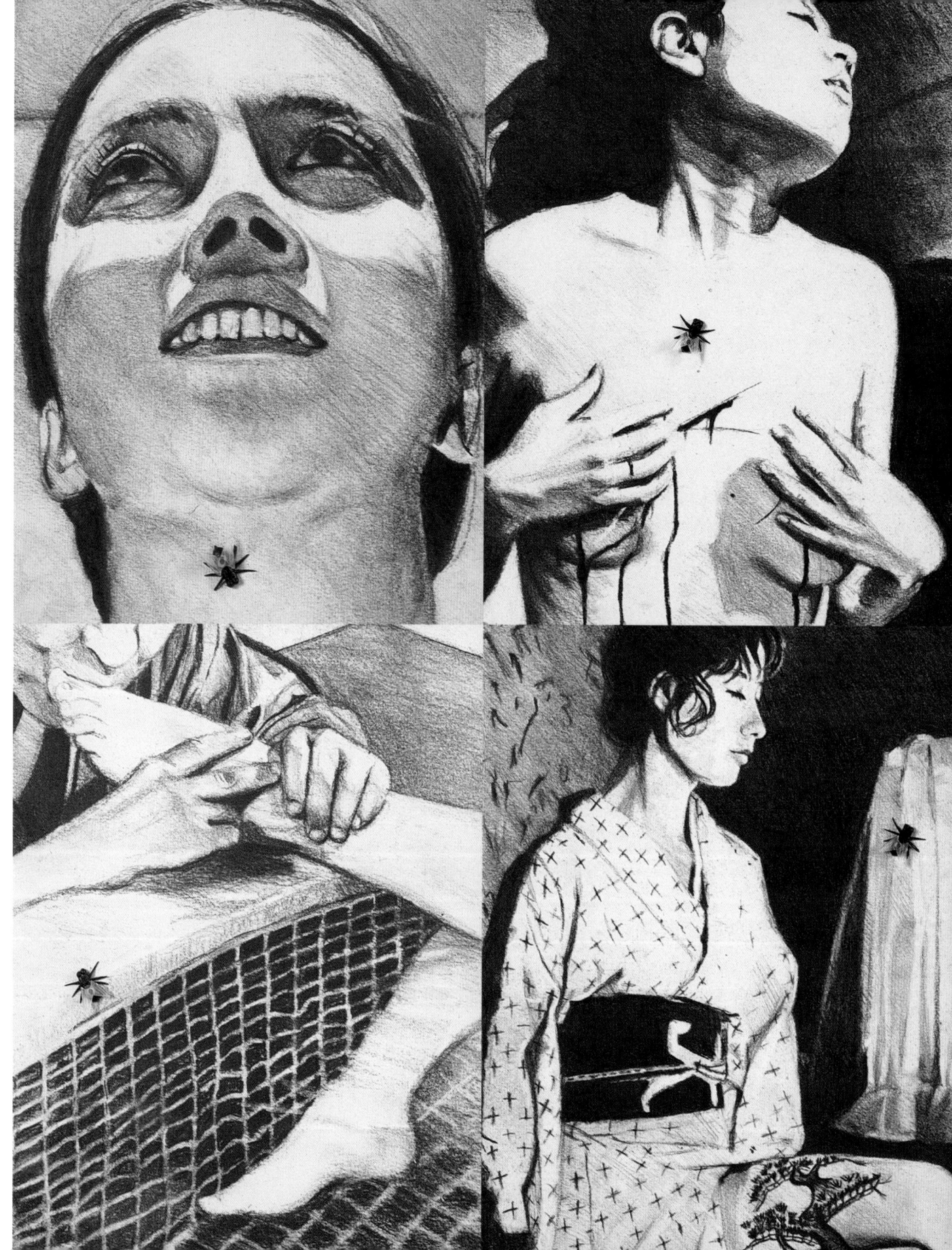

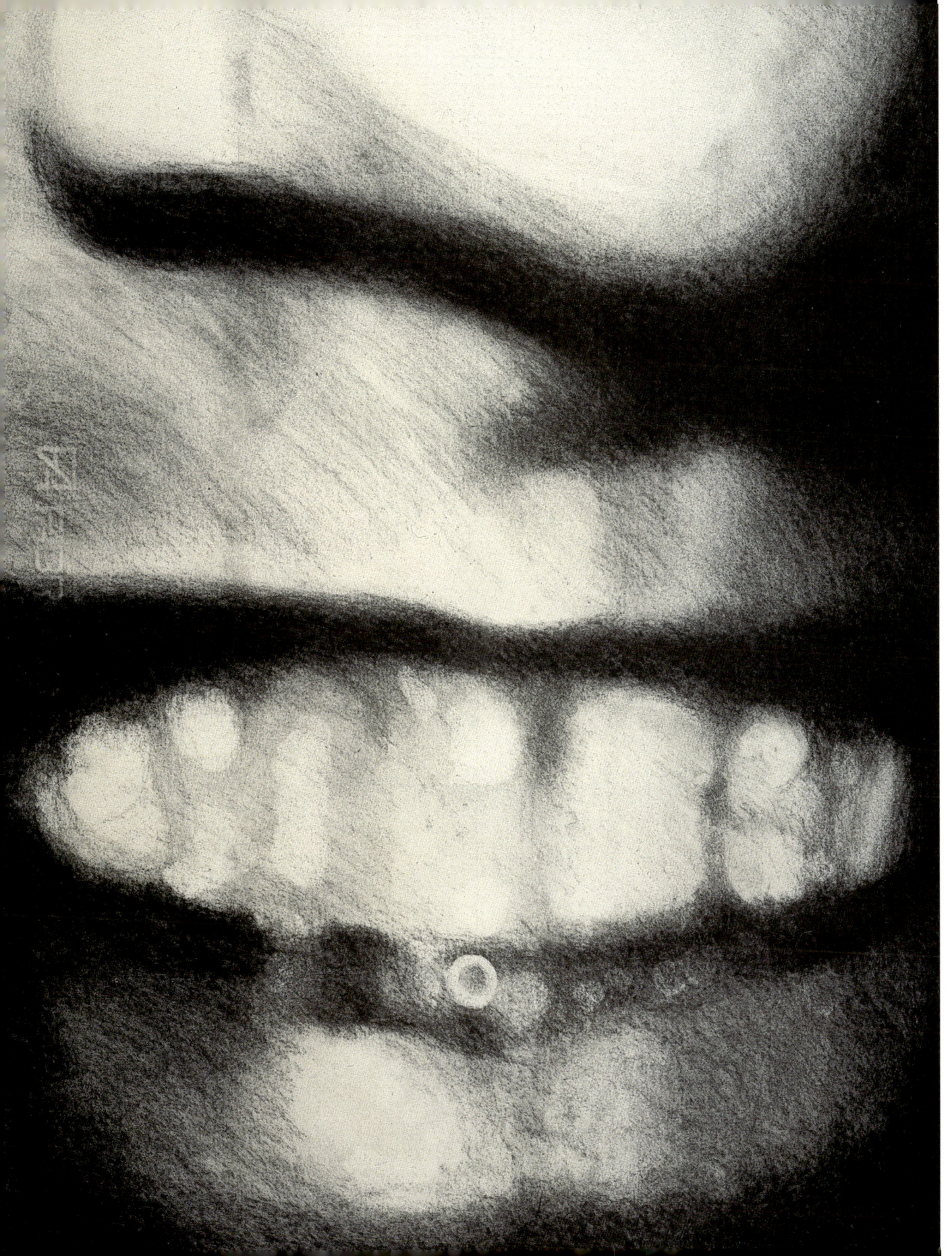

208-241 AMATEUR REFLEX

Japan has the most varied and vibrant publishing industry in Asia. It is said that the Japanese home market is so strong that it is possible to sustain itself without any need to export books abroad. One of the spin-off's of such a healthy publishing industry is the growth of vanity publishing, self-published volumes of work by Japan's many amateur writers, photographers and painters. Before World War II the art market in Japan was dominated by a conservative sensibility that concentrated on traditional forms of painting and illustration. After World War II that system collapsed leading to a number of artists expressing their views through self-publications. Even today and the Japanese art market is still in its infancy. Often self-published books provide an outlet for artists, providing them with the means of accessing a wider audience for their work. They also reveal a very different side to the Japanese psyche, one that is a combination of both Eastern and Western influences. They represent the fusion of an 'outsider sensibility' with an 'insider take' on Japanese culture. To this extent, the Japanese amateur market provides a unique insight into the self-contradictions of Japanese culture. They are indicators to a different Japan to the one known in the West.

210 Takeshi Shimajiri is an amateur photographer who has self-published many books depicting his own peculiar brand of portraiture, that of Japanese women, often dressed in traditional kimonos or bathing suits, yet always photographed with a phallic looking steam train in the distance.

218 Keisuke Shimizu's flat paintings of his family and friends are quintessentially Japanese in their choice of subject matter revealing a bizarre preoccupation with Western perspective coupled with a Japanese sensibility.

226 Shige Murakawa is a rare commodity in Japan, a Christian photographer whose self-published book under the pseudonym 'Kyrie Eleison' depicts young girls playing dead in real life interpretations of passages from the Bible. In the 19th century Japan was inundated with Western missionaries seeking converts and preaching the word of Christ. Today and the birth of Christ is loosely celebrated in Japan although Christmas Day is still a workday just like any other.

234 Sanichi Onozawa's raunchy paintings of Japanese strippers encapsulate the amateur aesthetic through his own appropriation of the expressionist palette. These paintings are a perfect example of Japanese outsider art at its best.

AMATEUR REFLEX　おのざわさんいち　SANACHI ONOZAWA

242-271 IMAGINED REFLEX

Since the end of World War II Japan has embraced Western consumerism and Western culture wholeheartedly. From celebrating the consumer festival of Christmas with carol singing and gifts to fast food joints with a Japanese twist, purchasing masterpieces of Western art or buying up vast tracks of Western real estate, the traditional values of Japan have become merged with a new set of consumerist and cultural aspirations. One of the key side effects of such cross-cultural pollination has been the questioning of what it means to be Japanese in the twentieth century. Many Japanese feel a sense of identity crisis when confronted with the reality of a nation that is both Western and Eastern in its influences. This sense of uncertainty has led many artists to produce work that questions both the imagined future of the Japanese psyche coupled with the question of self-identity. Yet the schizophrenic reality of the Japanese mindset is also a matter for celebration, making Japan culturally one of the most symbolically evolved nations in the world.

244 Miwa Yanagi's portraits of young Japanese teenagers are based on an on-going *Grandmother series* of work in which she asked Japanese youngsters to imagine their own futures as Grandmothers which she then dramatically recreates in a series of photographic prints.

254 Hiroyuki Matsukage's photographs of teenage fans interspersed with young girls holding beer or bottles of milk refer back to the language of advertising and its ability to transfer meaning through popular culture. Matsukage is himself a member of a music group in Japan called *Gorgerous* as well as working part-time in advertising.

262 Yasumasa Morimura is one of Japan's leading art world personalities whose work appropriates the language of Western culture. Personally appearing throughout his work in a variety of iconic guises, both male and female, his art rethinks the Western identity crisis embedded at the heart of Japan as well as Western culture itself.

SACHIKO

Even though I thought that I had become totally used to living alone by now, yesterday, no matter how hard I tried,
I just could not stand being in the house by myself.
It seemed as if the winter sunset had overtaken the entire world,
and was, little by little, scorching everything in its path.
I got up and drove to the airport, and, not surprisingly, got on the first airplane I could find.
I was trying to escape from the sun, but now I was the one chasing it.

Among all the skies I've seen so far, this is the most extraordinarily divine.
At this very moment, this is probably the most beautiful brightness.
Although I used to hope of dying while gazing upon such a heavenly sky,
My bearing witness to this brilliance right now makes my prior wish nothing but a trivial dream.

As I was about to depart from the airport, I called my friend Kimiko and told her that I was on my way...
and my, was she surprised!
Since I chose the airplane at random, my trip has encountered quite a detour.
I wonder how many hours it will take to get to Iviza via Singapore?
Until I reach that far away island where Kimiko resides, I shall surrender myself to the light.

独り暮しにはもうすっかり慣れたつもりなのに／昨日はどうしても一人で家に居られなかった
冬の夕焼けが世界中をおおいつくして／じりじりと焼きつくしてしまうようで
空港までドライブをしたら／そのまま飛行機に飛び乗ってしまった
でも太陽から逃げるつもりが／追いかけてしまったみたいね

今まで見た中でも、とびきり神々しい空／今この時、世界中で一番美しい光
死ぬ時は美しい空を見ながらなんて／思ったことがあったけど
この輝きを見ていると／私の願いなんて小さなものね

空港を発つとき／キミコに電話したら驚いてたわ
行き当たりで選んだ飛行機だから／随分遠回りになってしまった
シンガポール経由で／イビサ島まで何時間？
彼女の住む遥かな島まで／しばらく光に身を委ねて過ごしましょう

MIWA

Over the past ten years, I have looked after a great number of children.
Whenever I go out to meet one of my new offspring, we all end up going on a journey together.

"Having crossed 80 paths, it has become a challenge to traverse the mountains and the streams of the world.
Even the most remote corners of the globe, I know that my offspring are there to be found."

この10年で
多くの子達を引き取った。
新しい子を迎えに行くときは
必ず皆で旅をする。

八十路過ぎ幾山河越えるは難し
最果ての地にも我が子のあると思えば

AYUMI

Possibly due to the clear morning air,
I could hear the sound of water falling from a small waterfall close by.

"Pardon me, Sir, but are you awake?
Your breakfast has been prepared..."

"Ah."

"How was it, Sir?
Did Grandmother show you good dreams?"

" Thanks to being shown such a wonderful dream,
my body and mind have become completely relaxed.
By the way, is she always asleep like that?
Lying next to her while she is asleep is alright,
I guess, but can't I meet her when she is awake?"

"She cannot wake up, Sir. For your Grandmother is Sleeping Beauty."

朝の澄みきった空気のせいか、小さな滝の水音がさらに近くに聞こえた。

「お客様、お目覚めですか。朝食の支度ができてますけれど…」

「ああ。」

「いかがでしたか。祖母は良い夢を見せましたか?」

「いい夢を見させてもらって、身も心も軽くなった。ところで彼女はずっと眠ったままなの?

添い寝もいいが、起きてる彼女には会えないの?」

「目覚めません。祖母は「眠れる美女」ですから。」

私の生徒だったあなた達と、この島に流れ着いて十数年、
ここはもはや地球で唯一の場所なのか、
他に生き残った人間はいないのか、
知るすべもないままに、私たちは生き延びました。

私より長い未来を生きるあなたたちは、
将来、この島をでることがあるでしょうか。
異性や他の人間と会うことがあるのでしょうか。

たとえ最後の独りになっても生きていけるように
私はあなた達を育ててはきたけれど。

私の願いはただ一つ、
どうかこの島に住むすべての命が
次の世代を生むように。
地球の萌芽となりますように。

MIKA

It's been over ten years since you, my former students,
And I arrived on this island.
Is this already the last place on earth?
Are there no other survivors?
Without really knowing how, somehow we survived.

Compared to me, you will all lead long lives.
And in the future, you will probably leave this island, right?
You'll probably even meet members of the opposite sex
And other humans as well.

Even if you were the last human on earth,
I would raise you in a way that will go on.

I have only one wish...
That somehow all the life forms that live on this island
Give birth to the next generation.
May you all become the germinators of the world.

私の人生の初めの数十年で出会った人々は、親兄妹も夫も友人も
世界中の大部分の人々とともに死に絶えた。

あの災厄の数年のあと世界は一変した。人も都市も水底に消えた。
生き残った人々は、以前の世界を取り戻す事だけを願った。
多くの指導者や教祖が現れ、その争いは酸鼻を極めた。
いよいよ滅びが近づいたとき、僅かになった人間は
すべての過去を忘れ、共に生きる道を選んだ。

今、どの人間にも使命がある。
私は、近い将来この世界にやってくる困難を、この塔の中で予見するのが役目。
それぞれの集落に一人は予見者がいて、互いに助け合う事もあるが、私達は指導者ではない。
天災を予見しても防ぐ手立てがないことも多い。
今もどこかでまたひとつ集落が消滅するのが見えた。

死を悲しむ事もなく、新たな命の誕生に祝福はなく、何かを求めることもない。
わずかな糧を分かち合い、役目を果たせなくなれば自ら死を選ぶだけの事。

それでも人は生きられる。
完全な共存と平等が、ここにはある。

MIE

All of the people that I met in the first decades of my life, my parents, my brother, my sister, my husband, my friends, all of them, with most of the other people in the world, have met their end.

In the years after this great disaster, the world completely changed.
People... cities... everything... disappeared under the sea.
The survivors wished only for a return to the world as it once was. Many leaders and originators appeared on the scene, battles between the survivors raged on, plunging humanity into a disastrous state of affairs.
Day by day, as extinction drew nearer for the human race, the few remaining people of the world forgot everything from the past, and chose to follow the road leading to life and to survival hand-in-hand with one another.

Now, every human being has a mission in life. As for me, it is my duty to foresee the difficulties that shall face us as I peer out into the unknown from this mighty spire. Although each colony is home to one such seer, who in kind assists the others in our work, by no means are we the shepherds of the human race. No matter how many disasters we foretell, we lack the means by which to prevent them in the majority of cases.

To this day, we can see the disappearance of an entire colony at any time, in any place.

This is not something about lamenting over death, nor is it a blessing in the form of new life, in fact, it's not even something that we can pursue. It is however, about sharing what little remaining food we have left, and, should we become unable to carry out our given role, it is simply about choosing death for ourselves as a race.

And yet, we survive.
This is the place where perfect harmony and equality dwell.

REFLEX リフレックス

First published in Great Britain in 2003 by Trolley Limited,
Unit 5, Building 13, Long Street, London E2 8HN, UK.

Images © to the individual artists featured in this title
Text © Mark Sanders, 2003

Edited by Mark Sanders, Fumiya Sawa and Kyoichi Tsuzuki
Art Direction by Matt Roach

10 9 8 7 6 5 4 3 2 1

The right of authors to be identified as the authors of this work has been asserted by them in accordance with the Copyright, Designs and Patents Act 1998.

A catalogue record for this book is available from the British Library
ISBN 0-9542648-6-X

All rights reserved. No part of this publication may be reproduced, transmitted or stored in a retrieval system, in any form or by any means, without permission in writing from Trolley Limited, application for which must be made to Trolley Limited.

Printed in Hong Kong by Toppan

The editors of Reflex would like to thank the following people for their assistance in making this book possible.

Stephen Friedman Gallery (London)
Rika Fujiki at Mizuma Art Gallery (Tokyo)
Tomio Koyama Gallery (Tokyo)
Mokujisha
Asako Nanbu and Hisako Motoo at Matrix Inc
Galerie Emmanuel Perrotin (Paris)
Roentogen Gallery (Tokyo)
The Shiseido Gallery (Tokyo)
Kadokawa Shoten Publishing House
Satomi Yamaga
Michael Zink Gallery (München)
Blum & Poe (Los Angeles)
Marianne Boesky Gallery (New York)

Front cover + section breaks: manga girls courtesy of Gingashuppan
Kyupi Kyupi: Vermillion Pleasure Night
Kenji Yanobe photo credits: 126-133
Joel van Allmen
Vincent D. Feldman
Hideki Hiromoto
Shin Kurosawa
Tatsuhiko Nakagawa
Tadahisa Sakurai
Seiji Toyonaga

Special thanks: Akiko Ueda